They are here.

Copyright

The V3GA005 Are Coming
Life After Bacon

Copyright © 2026 Marcel Gerstel
www.TheVegansAreComing.com.au

Published by MindLoop
www.mindloop.com.au

ISBN 978-1-7640239-2-4
ABN 94 256 399 396
TVAC_IS_107_HUM-2026-03a

All rights reserved. No part of this publication may be reproduced, stored, or transmitted in any form or by any means – electronic, mechanical, photo-copying, recording, or otherwise – without prior written permission of the publisher, except as permitted by applicable copyright law.

This publication may challenge commonly held beliefs, shorten dinner conversations, and cause mild discomfort.

Satirical by design, it critiques systems, cultural practices, organisations, and industries – not individuals – as social commentary. Any resemblance to reality is, regrettably, intentional.

*Protein claim not verified by any known or meaningful authority.
Consume responsibly (and try not to lick the page).

Content

viii	....	Prologue
002	....	Vegans Ruined Everything
010	....	Sitting on Your High Horse
016	....	Salad Torture & Other Fantasies
022	....	Plant-Based... ish
028	....	Fishy Logic
034	....	Leafy Lies
040	....	A Bug's Life
046	....	Frankensnacks
052	....	The Big Meat Flex
058	....	Hard to Swallow
066	....	Green Outside, Grilled on the Inside
072	....	Bro-Science: In Protein We Trust
080	....	Buzz Buzz Buzz
088	....	The Lion Made Me Do It
094	....	Pampered Prisoners
100	....	Death Sticks & Dad Jokes
106	....	Meat Prescription
112	....	Planet of the Caged
120	....	Smoke Gets in Your Skies
128	....	Gambling on Legs
136	....	Eco-Justice: Reloaded
142	....	Mylk Wars
150	....	Feeding Frenzy
158	....	Shell Shock
166	....	Udder Nonsense
174	....	The Silence of the Ham
180	....	The Kid's Menu
186	....	Future News Headline
190	....	On Numbers and Other Distractions
192	....	To Those Who Lit the Fire (Credits)

V

To the animals who never grew up.

PROLOGUE – The Things We Love to Eat

(Or: How to hug a cow and still order the burger.)

We live in the golden age of moral gymnastics. Compassion trends on Mondays, outrage on Wednesdays, and by Friday we're elbow-deep in a bucket of chicken nuggets, whispering, "Treat yourself. You deserve it".

We'll stop traffic for a dog, call it a hero act, then drive past a truck full of pigs on the way to *processing* – which, by the way, is the nicest word ever invented for industrialised, mechanised dismemberment.

We cry at rescue videos, hashtag empathy, then upload our dinner plate like it's a hostage photo with garnish.

Kindness is now a lifestyle brand. Cruelty is a subscription service that auto-renews through Uber Eats.

We donate to koalas while eating cows. We save dolphins, then eat tuna – a moral logic equivalent to building a lifeboat for one passenger while deliberately drilling holes in the boats carrying the rest.

We raise dogs like children, cats like royalty, and pigs like bacon. The distinction is simple: domesticate or marinate. Some we tame and name. Others we beat, then eat.

Our vocabulary works overtime to keep the conscience quiet. We don't kill – we *process*. We don't steal babies – we *separate calves*. We don't torture – we *test for safety*. Somewhere, there's a marketing intern who got a promotion for turning 'pain and suffering' into 'farm-to-table'.

Along the way, *vegan* got tangled up with *plant-based* – one being a diet, the other a moral position that somehow became the awkward relative everyone avoids at family gatherings.

Marketers – bless their chlorophyll-soaked hearts – decided *vegan* sounded snappier. And they weren't entirely wrong. But the side effect is this: you can now eat a salad, bet on horse races, and buy leather shoes without so much as a hiccup of moral indigestion.

These are two different things. One is about what goes in your mouth. The other is about what lives in your head.

This isn't a personal failing – it's a successful marketing campaign, erasing empathy one person at a time.

We've been gently lied to, professionally reassured, and carefully trained to accept the most unnatural behaviours as everyday routine. Not because we're cruel, but because someone figured out how to make cruelty feel normal, invisible and very profitable.

And still, the question sneaks in between mouthfuls: If we really love animals, why do we eat the ones who never asked to be our special dinner guest? (And no, mumbling something about the *circle of life* doesn't get us out of this – it's a Disney jingle, not a moral philosophy).

We tell ourselves bedtime stories so we can sleep through breakfast. That it's natural. That they don't feel pain. That bacon smells like home. We've stretched *humane* so far it could double as a resistance band in a Pilates class.

This book won't give you purity. It gives you honesty – the kind that burns a little going down but might also clear your arteries of denial.

It's a mirror. A slightly cracked one – fun-house warped – but if you squint, you'll still recognise the species responsible.

A rare collection of notes, rants, and quiet moments of disbelief about how a species capable of so much empathy also invented industrial suffering, packaged it efficiently, and called it normal.

The real trick wasn't hiding the truth – it was convincing us we'd never need to look.

Out of sight, out of empathy.

Out of empathy, out of consequence.

Maybe the real question isn't whether we *can* live without exploiting animals – it's why we ever thought we couldn't.

Being vegan was never about swapping cow's milk for oat milk. It was about swapping apathy for empathy. The oat milk just makes it easier to swallow.

The funny part – and no one advertises this – is that change doesn't actually begin with doing something dramatic. No Lycra. No yoga mat. No sudden urge to buy a bicycle that costs more than your car.
Sometimes it starts with just *not* doing something.

Walking past a product instead of picking it up. Not negotiating with it like an ex who wants another chance. Just leaving it there – untouched – and realising that restraint can be a surprisingly effective form of rebellion.

Let's begin. Together. With empathy.

The
VEGANS
Are Coming

Life After Bacon

Unfiltered. Unfinished. Unapologetic. Unmeatable.

C. K. Gerstel

Vegans Ruined Everything

AKA: Attack of the Kale People

(How compassion got rebranded as radical extremism.)

Dumb Scale	
Fixability Index	
Outrage Level	

The Situation

Somewhere in the cultural basement – right next to a dusty box labelled 'Common Sense (2003–2011)' – the people of this world collectively decided that 'vegan' wasn't merely a diet or an ethical position. It was a *provocation*. A threat. A personal insult wrapped in kale and dusted with nutritional yeast.

The moment someone casually says, "Actually, I don't eat animals", society reacts like a toddler being told Santa isn't real. Tantrums follow. Jokes fly. Eyes roll.

And somehow, the person with the salad becomes the villain – in a story written by barbecue enthusiasts and peer-reviewed by Uncle Terry, who holds a great interest in the subject of Bacon Studies.

You'd think someone refusing to participate in hurting animals would be the mildest act of rebellion ever imaginable. But oh no. In the grand theatre of modern identity politics, choosing tofu is apparently an extremist move.

Vegans became the punchline that keeps insecure omnivores warm at night – like a cosy heated blanket powered entirely by denial.

The irony? Nobody hates vegans more than someone who suspects vegans might... actually have a point.

The human conscience is sensitive – poke it gently and it screams like you kicked it in the shins. Which is exactly why the backlash arrived with humour as armour and memes as camouflage.

Why It's Ridiculous

Ah yes, the Greatest Hits:

- **Plants feel pain**

  A claim we've already given an entire chapter somewhere in this book more patience than it deserved.

- **Humans have always eaten meat**

  So? People also lick frozen lamp posts, and used to think the sun revolved around them and that shouting at the night sky might help with the weather.

- **Vegans are trying to cancel meat-eaters**
  If only vegans could cancel chicken wings at a family gathering.

This entire backlash is wrapped up guilt, pretending to be logic. A moral hangover disguised as common sense. When someone says, "I'm vegan", people don't hear the words – they hear the echo of their own conscience mumbling, "We *could* do better".

So instead of wrestling with that discomfort, they weaponise punchlines. Roast the vegan before the vegan can make you think. Works every time.

But hold on – plot twist incoming. The vegan hate machine didn't emerge organically. No grassroots uprising, no spontaneous eye-roll festival. No. It was *curated*, seasoned, slow-fermented. And here it is: the vegan hate machine isn't organic – it's *sponsored*.

Now this may be mildly unsettling for some folks, so occasionally – just to make the whole thing feel less theoretical – someone actually slips in and admits this part out loud.

An anonymous insider, bound by the kind of paperwork that ensures silence without technically requiring it, recently described being paid to *blend in* online. Not to argue against veganism directly – that's inefficient – but to *exaggerate* it. To push the most alienating takes. To derail discussions with purity tests, edge cases, and moral dead-ends.

Not to defeat vegan ideas – but to make vegans look foolish and unbearable.

No names. No finger-pointing. Just a description so mundane it barely counts as a scandal. Because if you've ever watched a social media comment section collapse under the weight of mosquito ethics or backyard egg discourse, you already know how effective that strategy is.

You don't need to silence a movement if you can make it argue with itself in public and burn out from within.

The meat and dairy industries spend millions painting vegans as humourless extremists. Because if you think someone's ridiculous, you'll never listen to them.

It's PR 1-0-1: when you can't refute the message, just set the messenger on fire – preferably with sizzling bacon memes.

So vegans were rebranded as the fun police of food. And suddenly, every insecure omnivore was handed a playbook, a script to feel safe again. 'Bacon though'. 'I could never give up cheese'. 'I respect your choice, but...'

It wasn't accidental – it was *marketing*. The same kind of marketing that once told women cigarettes were glamorous and empowering. That it calmed the nerves and that a relaxed mother was a good mother – and if a doctor appeared in the ad, even better.

Different product. Same routine. Repackage harm as freedom. Sell reassurance. Mock anyone who suggests otherwise. Next.

How to Un-F*ck It

- **Recognise the knee-jerk**
  If the word 'vegan' raises your heart rate, you're *reacting* – not reasoning.
- **Let guilt breathe**
  It's not an insult; it's your moral conscience standing on your shoulder, waving a tiny, little flag that says, "Hellooo. Are you listening to this?'
- **Retire the propaganda**
  The 'crazy vegan' stereotype didn't develop without help – it was *manufactured*, like a fast-food patty. And most people swallowed it without even reading the label.
  Next time... Read. The. Label.
- **Get curious, not defensive**
  The V-word isn't an insult. You *can* ask 'why' without building a fortress and bringing out the troops.
- **Stop doing free marketing for Big Bacon**
  At this point, the 'bacon though' crowd should at least receive a Christmas hamper for its loyalty.

Leaving You With This
(Scientifically robust, philosophically deep, and comically needless.)

If vegans were really plotting to cancel meat-eaters, they're doing a terrible job. Most can't even cancel their aunt's passive-aggressive lamb roast jokes.

The only thing vegans have ever successfully cancelled is the occasional friendship, family closeness and their own appetite – usually after learning how hot dogs are made. And if that information doesn't ruin *your* lunch, nothing ever will.

Image Of Vandalism
(Sententia Contaminata)
Public restroom ceramic tile wall inscription in black marker ink.
An ethical statement and its refusal share the same surface.
The wall continues to serve its original function.

Sitting on Your High Horse

AKA: Galloping Boldly Into Bullsh*t

(Humans, horses, and the art of dressing cruelty as culture.)

Dumb Scale
Fixability Index
Outrage Level

The Situation

We, carbon-based life-forms, were gifted legs. Two of them. A buy-one-get-one-free deal. We invented the wheel. We invented cars, trains, planes, and whatever fever dream Elon's launching next.

And yet some people still say: "Nah, I'll just sit on the exposed spine of this other animal and make it haul my lazy arse around". Few things scream dominant species like looking at a gentle herbivore and thinking, "Yep... that'll carry me".

Why It's Ridiculous

You weigh eighty kilos, and the silence beneath your butt shouldn't be assumed as agreement.

It's marketed as 'sport'. Wealthy humans watch other humans sit on the back of a horse to see whose animal can look most stressed while jumping over sticks.

'Nostalgia' is the favourite excuse. "It's tradition", they say – so were a lot of things we're now quietly embarrassed by.

Efficiency? Try feeding, grooming, housing, and shoeing a horse. Then compare it to putting petrol in a 1987 Corolla held together by zip ties.

And lets not even go near the trail riding holiday – or better known as "Come and relax by strapping yourself to half a ton of nervous anxiety with hooves that panics at the sight of a windblown plastic bag".

The Delusion Beneath the Saddle

Now, let's be honest to ourselves, it's not really about the horse, is it? It's about the illusion. An ancient fantasy where a certain kind of human casts themselves as noble warriors, or beach-riding Disney princesses. Always in slow motion. Always toward a sunset. Always with three filters and a caption explaining why this feels profound.

Why You Should Care

Horses suffer chronic back pain, joint damage, and stress, all for the human vanity.

People of all sizes bounce around in black crash helmets, protecting their egos just in case the 600kg creature decides to navigate itself.

Entire industries exist to normalise animal exploitation as 'sport' or 'artistic'. It's wildly expensive, exclusive, and socially celebrated – another reminder that cruelty, when served with champagne and a hat shaped like a fruit salad, can still be mistaken for respectability.

It's humanity refusing to admit an embarrassing truth: we evolved to walk – and then outsourced that responsibility to a creature whose purpose in life we decided long ago.

How to Un-F*ck It

- Retire the horses. Let them eat grass and gossip with cows about donkeys.
- Equestrian sports? Replace with Human Jumping Competitions – bring back dignity to sport: pull up your socks, enjoy some leather strapping, attempt a water jump, and discover new muscles and regrets – all within less than 2 minutes.
- Introduce the **WYOA** *(Walk Your Own Arse)* act: if your legs work, you are required to use them.
- Museums of Transportation must include a display labelled: 'Horse Riding: A Historical Case Study in Load-Induced Animal Injury'.

- Luxury horse ownership taxed at 200% – all proceeds go to improve public transport. Any owner complaining about the tax must report in person to the complaint counter to receive an additional 50% on top of their fine.

Leaving You With This
(Scientifically approved, philosophically verified, and entirely unasked for.)

Letting another animal walk for you when your own legs work perfectly fine is peak human idiocracy: too proud to walk, too stubborn to change, too blind to notice the limp beneath them.

Time to dismount, dust off the dignity, apologise to the horse, and remember the ability of putting one foot in front of the other.

WTF But True

The Australian Melbourne Cup – 'The Race That Stops a Nation'. Or, more accurately known as 'The Race That Stops a Horse's Heart'.

Nothing screams Aussie culture like a $12 champers, served in a plastic flute, destined to outlive the winning horse.

Meanwhile, thousands in formal costumes and foolish-looking headwear slide into the mud, running a national sweepstake on which animal collapses first, before wrapping up the day's spectacle by being trolleyed into the nearest bottle-o.

Raise a glass to *Verema, Admire Rakti, Araldo, Red Cadeaux, The CliffsofMoher,* and *Anthony Van Dyck* – not the fallen heroes we deserved, but the ones we ignored.

Against All Odds

In 2022, Melbourne formally banned horse-drawn carriages from the CBD after years of public pressure.

No more horses dodging trams, taxis, and tourists on Swanston Street – they've finally been upgraded from bumper-barriers to grass.

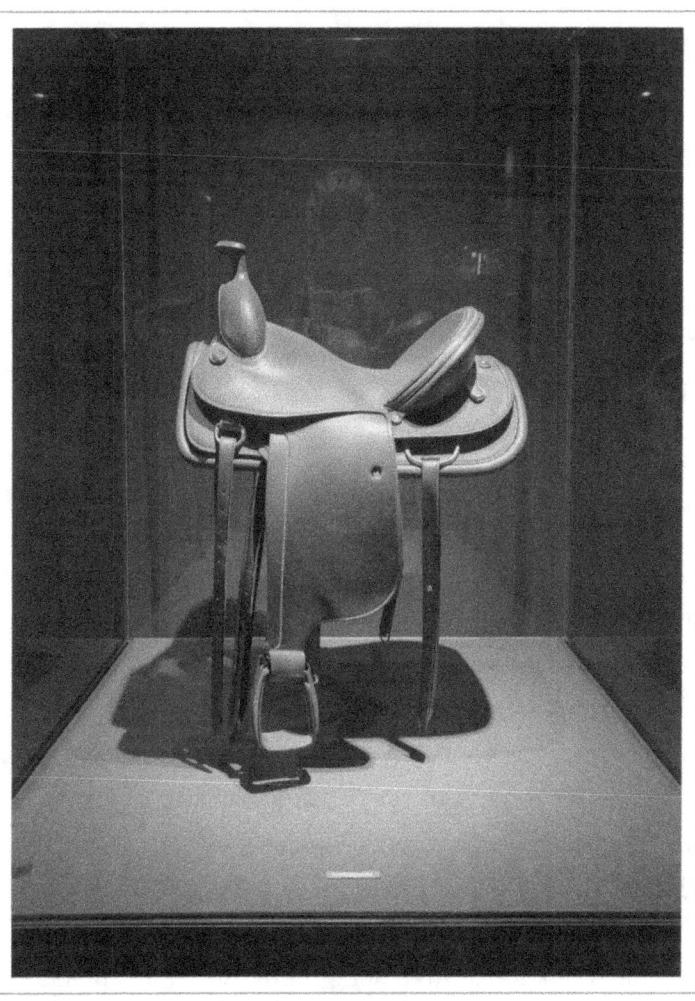

Riding Saddle
(Onus Delegatum)
Device used to position a human body on a horse.
Facilitates load bearing and directional control
for transportation, recreation, or sport.
Voluntary participation of the animal is not a considered parameter.

Salad Torture & Other Fantasies

AKA: A Tragedy in Three Salads

(The complete loss of common sense.)

Dumb Scale
Fixability Index
Outrage Level

The Situation

Humanity, endlessly proud of its well deserved progress, in its quest to out-weird itself, invented spray-on cheese, leaf blowers and the idea that broccoli somehow feels distressed when being sliced.

Every vegan eventually has to hear the panicked battle cry of someone halfway through a steak, losing the argument:

"BUT PLANTS FEEL PAIN!"

Said with the confidence of a man who hasn't opened a science book since high school but suddenly speaks fluent photosynthesis.

The argument suggests: If carrots suffer, then eating cows is fine. Of course – everyone understands this isn't an argument but complete nonsense – and nobody actually believes it.

But let's clear this up anyway: plants don't have brains, nerves, or anything that even remotely resembles pain receptors – nor do they have any emotional capacity to resent your cutlery.

They also don't form emotional attachments, write shitty pop songs, or keep football scores. Evolution just didn't equip them to bend that way.

What they *do* have are chemical signalling systems – biology's version of automated responses, not consciousness. But that's not pain; that's biochemistry doing its job. A plant responding to stimuli isn't agony; it's biological engineering.

Yeah, yeah, yeah, plants fire off tiny electrical pulses – but so does an old fridge or your Nan's 1960s transistor radio, and no one's worried about hurting its feelings when they change the station.

If you think your spinach is screaming, that's not science. That's the sound of a bad argument failing – embarrassingly.

Why It's Ridiculous

Picture this: a crowd of adults – partially educated and historically indifferent to suffering – suddenly trembling over the emotional well-being of a cucumber. They'll argue that slicing celery might be murder –

while chewing on a cheeseburger the size of a grown chihuahua.

If plants really did feel pain, the logical response would be to eat *fewer* of them – which also means... ditching the steak. Since livestock eat most of the world's soy and grains, your bacon breakfast killed far more plants than a block of tofu ever will.

So, the entire argument backfires harder than a diesel ute on cheap fuel. Even in an alternate universe where lettuce had feelings, it'd probably prefer a quick harvest over a lifetime stuck in a feedlot listening to corporate jingles on loop and waiting to be extruded into a nugget.

Why You Should Care

The 'plants feel pain' defence isn't about plants or pain. It's all about the moral get-out-of-jail-free card people toss on the table when real empathy becomes cornered.

It's cognitive dissonance hiding behind flora fluff. A desperate attempt to drag the moral bar so low it's ready to grow roots.

No one truly believes broccoli is crying. They just need broccoli to play dead long enough to win the argument and shut that pesky vegan up.

How to Un-F*ck It

- **Photosynthesis awareness program**
  Teach people what sunlight actually does before they confuse chemistry with cruelty.
- **Install the Pain-O-Meter™**
  If it doesn't have a brain, nerves, or legs to run away with, it's probably fine.
- **Rename meat production 'Plant Murder'**
  And suddenly watch the argument detonate like a tomato in a blender.
- **Launch a CSI: *Salad Victims Unit***
  Dedicated to solving cases where no victim is present.

Leaving You With This
(Scientifically slippery, philosophically sticky, and spiritually gooey.)

Plants: the chillest citizens on Earth. Turning sunlight into sugar since forever, minding their own business, and never asking for anything except water – and perhaps not to be dragged into human conversations about ethics.

WTF But True

Over 80% of global soy goes straight into livestock feed. So anyone sincerely worried about soybean suffering could spare the innocent bean fastest by stopping its conversion into pigs, poultry, and weekend barbecues.

And yes – scientists have recorded some plant vibrations under stress, but calling that 'pain' is like worrying your WiFi is suffering when your phone drops out.

Against All Logic

In 2021, a wellness guru announced he had stopped eating plants to 'avoid harming them'. He shifted to breatharianism – a slightly different term for 'starving yourself' – but delivered with the utmost confidence.

Broccoli
(Brassica oleracea var. italica)
Cut plant specimen. Commercial food crop.
Frequently referenced in discussions
equating plant harvesting with animal suffering.
No neurological structures associated with pain responses are present.
The claim remains in circulation.

Plant-Based... Ish

AKA: Moral Gymnastics in Yoga Pants

(Compassion – just not on weekends, holidays, or when it's inconvenient.)

Dumb Scale
Fixability Index
Outrage Level

The Situation

Welcome to the Age of Flexible Morality – where ethics come with trial periods, moral decisions ship with cheat codes, and compassion is something you squeeze in between brunch and episode six.

The modern dietary spectrum now reads less like a philosophy and more like a sitcom pitch:

Everybody's Trying, Nobody's Committing.

Behold, the great word-cluster of Dietary Identification:

- **Vegan**
  Eats plants. Sleeps at night.
- **Vegetarian**
  Loves animals – just not enough to avoid eggs, cheese, milk, honey, and whatever else still feels acceptable this afternoon.

- **Pescetarian**
  A morally enhanced omnivore; empathy applies to selected mammals only.
- **Flexitarian**
  Soul says compassion, stomach says 'meh'.
- **Reducetarian**
  A little harm reduction, loosely enforced.
- **Veganuary Survivor**
  Brags about enlightenment for exactly 31 days; then quietly reverts to old habits and cracks open a can of tuna.
- **Omnivore**
  Eats everything; questions nothing.
- **Chegan**
  Vegan... until tequila kicks the door in and shouts, **"WHO WANTS NACHOS?"**
- **Megan**
  Once ordered a vegan burger by mistake. Still talks about it.

Everybody's 'mostly vegan' now – which is like being 'mostly faithful'. Admirable, but entirely missing the point.

When someone sighs, "I'm doing my best", what they often mean is: "I've handed over my conscience to convenience, and my convenience has a terrible work ethic".

The world is full of those who want the moral high ground – just not the whole climb. One foot in ethics, the other ankle-deep in barbecue sauce.

It's the same energy as cancelling your gym membership and still telling your friends you identify as *active*.

Why It's Ridiculous

Ethics don't have cheat days. When suffering becomes optional, morality becomes cosmetic.

Imagine a judge who upholds the law – most days. Or a surgeon who saves who they can – whenever it's convenient. We would never tolerate selective duty in public life – yet excuse it entirely in private morality.

Somehow, society started to applaud dietary half-measures, mistaking intention for impact.

Occasional harm doesn't become ethical because it's framed as 'moderation'.

We've learned how to rename contradictions until they feel acceptable. Flexitarian isn't a new ethic – it's omnivorism spelled differently.

This is the age of Ethical Tourism – people wandering through morality like it's a weekend farmers market: browse a little compassion, buy nothing and go home with a sausage roll.

The world doesn't need eight billion almost-ethical humans. It needs fewer people treating morality as something they do only when it suits.

How to Un-F*ck It

- **Stop grading yourself on a moral curve**
  Outcomes are what matter.
- **Ditch the labels**
  You don't need a dietary identity – you need a functioning compass that doesn't change direction when temptation does.
- **Consistency beats convenience**
  It's that thing you do when no one's watching.
- **Remember**
  Almost ethical *isn't* ethical.

Leaving You With This
(Scientifically stamped, philosophically sealed, and socially unnecessary.)

Imagine this kind of morality as a first dinner date: flowers in one hand, a knife hidden behind the back.

We're proud of the flowers. We talk about the flowers. We photograph the flowers. The knife, conveniently ignored, keeps cutting.

Restaurant Menu Cover
Printed menu displaying dietary preference symbols.
Multiple dietary positions are represented through iconography.
Ethical, cultural, and health considerations are categorised for display.

Fishy Logic

AKA: SAVE THE FISH, EAT THE FISH

(The banning of the bendy straw.)

Dumb Scale
Fixability Index
Outrage Level

The Situation

Picture it: a waterfront restaurant where the ocean breeze is thick with irony. The menu flirts with phrases like 'line-caught', 'sustainably sourced', 'ocean-fresh'.

You order the grilled snapper because the waiter assures you it's 'ethically sourced' and 'ocean-friendly', which is restaurant-speak for "trust me bro".

It arrives with lemon, a decorative smear of green something, and a biodegradable bamboo straw in your Mojito. Plastic straws kill fish, you see.

The fish on your plate? That's a separate matter. That's dinner. Please respect the separation.

Why It's Ridiculous

Plastic straw in drink? 'Monster'.

Fishing nets the size of small neighbourhoods scraping the seafloor like gigantic Roombas of death? 'Standard operational gear'.

Turtle with a straw up its nose? Viral heartbreak; global outrage.

Tuna in tacos? "Relax, sweetheart – they used that dolphin-affirming aioli".

Seafood festival with no straws? "We saved the ocean, Bev!"

Meanwhile... the ocean is in the background howling like a whale who ran out of plankton.

The Real Problem

Ghost nets – abandoned industrial traps – make up nearly *half* of all ocean plastic. Kilometres of synthetic death drifting around like haunted laundry, strangling anything with fins, flippers, wings, curiosity, optimism or the misfortune of existing today.[1]

But sure... ban the bendy straw. Now *that* will really show those seabirds who's boss.

Why You Should Care

Symbolic eco-gestures let us dodge responsibility. We get to feel enlightened while changing precisely ...nothing.

---

1 Animal welfare is our top priority.

Straws? Less, *far less* than one percent of the problem. Fishing gear? *That's* the floating apocalypse nobody wants printed on their reusable coffee cup.

Legislation happily bans your frappé straw while letting a 70-kilometre drift net wipe out more dolphins before breakfast than Sea World could fit in it's tanks in a year.

Humanity has once again perfected environmentalism that photographs beautifully and achieves absolutely bugger-all.

How to Un-F*ck It

- **Seafood restaurant ethics test**
  Before ordering seafood, diners take a one-question quiz: "Which kills more marine life: straws or fishing?" Wrong answer? Dry kale salad. No dressing. Sit with it.

- **Ghost-Net-Garnish™**
  Each dish finished with a twist of recycled, premium grade fishing net, because it's already in the ocean anyway. Flavour is fleeting but the guilt and consequences can be with you forever.

- **Menu honesty labels**
  'By-catch not included (but guaranteed). Details unsuitable for children. Served on reclaimed deck-wood from the source vessel'.

- **Plastic-straw redemption tokens**
  Return five straws removed from the ocean for one mildly guilt-free seaweed-and-rice arrangement. *(Terms and conditions apply.)*

Leaving You With This
(Scientifically approved, philosophically confused, and morally outsourced.)

Humanity loves the symbolism of the straw because the straw can't stare back. Fish can. Or could.

WTF But True

- Around 40% of global fish catch is by-catch – turtles, dolphins, sharks, seabirds, and anything else unlucky enough to be alive there that day.
- 46% of the Great Pacific Garbage Patch is abandoned fishing gear. Not cups. Not bags. Nets.
- Straws? 0.03%. Statistically indistinguishable from a collective shrug.

Against All Odds

Tiny island nations doing the heavy lifting while seafood-devouring continents pat themselves on the back for banning small plastic cocktail ticklers.

- Seychelles converted national debt into marine sanctuaries – trading financial liability for ecological survival.

- Palau protected 80% of its waters by banning commercial fishing outright.

Ocean protection, it turns out, works best when the ocean *isn't* on the menu.

Industrial Fishing Net *(Fragment)*
(Instrumentum Extractionis)
Synthetic fibre netting used in commercial fishing operations.
Designed for large-scale capture of marine life.
Displays wear consistent with prolonged deployment.
Capture occurs without distinction.

Leafy Lies

AKA: Farm Fresh, Forest Dead

(When 'chemical-free' means 'tree-free'.)

Dumb Scale
Fixability Index
Outrage Level

The Situation

'Organic' was supposed to be the earth whispering sweet nothings through spinach leaves – the sort of image that makes any hippy briefly levitate.

In aisle three, someone clutches a reusable tote bag like a moral shield, radiating virtue onto their ethically massaged parsley.

Except... the math. Oh, the math.

Because the numbers don't care about your tote bag.

Organic standards prohibit synthetic fertilisers and pesticides. Great. Heroic. Medal-worthy. Until you notice the price: more land to grow the same food. That's not a compromise; that's agriculture mugging the rainforest behind the shops.

Forty to one hundred percent *more* land. That is not farming – that's a slow-motion decimation of the nearest forest.

For anyone mid-bite on a $7 organic tomato: a forest paid the bill. Something fluffy lost its lease. All so your salad could feel a little more spiritually moisturised in front of strangers.

Why It's Ridiculous

That glowing organic apple? It may have displaced a tree that once hosted an endangered bird's entire family history.

More land means more steel, more noise, more habitat quickly erased – efficiency worthy of someone who really shouldn't be trusted with wildlife decisions.

Organic is starting to resemble agriculture's boutique brand: premium pricing, comforting narratives, and a label that assumes you won't ask any follow-up questions.

The packaging says 'wholesome'. The numbers strongly disagree.

Why You Should Care

- **Deforestation**
  Whole ecosystems cleared so we can market lettuce and spinach as 'low-impact'.
- **Biodiversity collapse**
  Wildlife displaced or erased so carrots can be labelled 'sustainable'.
- **Extra emissions**
  Land clearing is not an environmentally benign process.
- **Opportunity cost**
  Every hectare locked into organic production is a hectare not returning to habitat.

We need to understand that those green labels don't change brown outcomes.

How to Un-F*ck It

- **Think vertical, not horizontal**
  Glowing LED towers, hydroponics, controlled-environment agriculture – farming that looks like a 1980's nightclub for lettuce. Up to 95% less land required. Food that grows *up* instead of *out*.

- **Urban farming**
  Food closer to people. Less transport. Less waste. Fewer avocados clocking up long-haul miles like tiny green jet-setters chasing frequent-flyer miles.
- **Tech over branding**
  A solar-powered greenhouse outperforms compost mysticism every day of the week ending in 'y' and twice on farmers' market days.
- **Redefine 'organic'**
  - Organic *isn't* pure.
  - Organic is *not* closer to nature.
  - Organic is *less* efficient.
  - Organic means *more* habitats flattened, more "sorry little buddy" moments for species that didn't get a say.

Organic farming doesn't eliminate harm. It *relocates* it – usually into forests, grasslands, and whatever was living there before the green tick on the label arrived.

Organic stepped away from poison. Vertical agriculture moves beyond both, poison *and* land hunger.

Leaving You With This
(Scientifically crunchy, philosophically chewy, and totally indigestible.)

The future of food won't be a hipster in hemp overalls hand-watering radishes on land that used to be a rainforest.

It will look closer to Blade Runner: rows of glowing green towers, quietly humming, "no forests were harmed in the making of this smoothie".

Nostalgia is comfortable. It's also spectacularly bad at feeding eight billion mouths.

WTF But True

If the entire planet went organic, we'd need roughly another Australia worth of farmland – plus a bonus New Zealand – just to garnish your sandwich.

Against All Odds

The Netherlands – a country roughly the size of a damp tea towel – is somehow the world's #2 food exporter, armed with high-tech greenhouses welded onto sensible principles.

Low land use. Low water use. High yield. Proof that efficiency and environmental restraint are not mutually exclusive.

Insect Sticky Trap
(Selectio Virtuosa)
Adhesive capture surface used in organic farming practices.
Immobilises insects for monitoring and control.
Capture occurs indifferent to insect species.

A Bug's Life

AKA: Meat, but Crunchier

(When future food is just yesterday's marketing on mushrooms.)

Dumb Scale
Fixability Index
Outrage Level

The Situation

Despite decades of nutritional data to the contrary, the thoroughly studied non-issue of 'protein deficiency' resurfaces every few years as a carefully manufactured panic.

But fear not. A new solution has arrived: Crickets!

Ground into powder, branded with a leaf-shaped logo, and embedded in snack bars – the eco-saviour of the decade, according to the label.

It sounds edgy. Futuristic even. Like a corporate vision of the future. In reality, it's 98% marketing and 2% crawly.

Protein has never been the problem. Lentils, peas, soy, hemp, quinoa, seaweed – the whole cast of characters sitting quietly in your pantry, waiting their turn.

So why push bugs?

Because if the world realises plants are enough, the meat and dairy narrative face-plants harder than a tipsy race-day punter in stilettos. The perfect decoy – the 'New Meat' that lets the Old Meat keep smoking behind the shed and we can pretend it's not a problem.

Why It's Ridiculous

We're starting to normalise killing *billions* of insects instead of... you know, simply not killing things at all.

It's legacy meat logic, still insisting: "If it once twitched, it counts as protein".

Insects don't scream – not audibly, anyway – but they're still very much alive. And the future of protein already exists. It's beans. It's always been beans. Shakespeare even tried to warn us: "To Bean or Not to Bean". Humanity unfortunately chose the 'not'.

Why You Should Care

Now, here's the sneak attack no one saw coming: Insect protein doesn't challenge meat culture; it *protects* it – a counter-punch aimed squarely at veganism.

The meat and dairy industries know fully well that plants are gaining ground (pun intended). They're terrified – not of tofu, but of its simplicity – which makes the entire debate unnecessary.

So along scuttles the cricket: "Look! An alternative protein! See? You don't need to go vegan, just eat this bug. It still feels like eating an animal.

It's a two-for-one special for the industry:

- Keep cultural dominance by maintaining the myth that protein must come from something that had legs or wiggled.
- Create the perfect straw-man: "You want us to stop eating steak and eat bugs instead? Nah mate – you vegans are insane!"
- The bug hype derails the plant-based movement just as it's gaining speed and it creates a whole new exploitation industry.
- Research money has moved disastrously away from algae, seaweed, duckweed, hemp, and legumes, the stuff that could actually save our species from turning the planet into a preheated oven.

All to keep the protein panic alive – a propaganda lovingly preserved. A panic, one might add, that's never really existed outside a brochure on the gym counter, wedged between the supplement shelf and the testosterone gummy bears.

How to Un-F*ck It

- **Fund plants, not bugs**
  Pour R&D into algae farms, spirulina, legumes, hemp, and seaweed – not cricket factories where a lifetime lasts hours.
- **Teach the obvious**
  "Plants Have Protein. Duh". Put it on billboards. Print it on cereal boxes. Project it onto Parliament House. Tattoo it on the Minister for Agriculture if necessary.
- **Label the basics**
  Make lentil and pea packaging shout their protein content the way protein powder does.
- **Policy levers**
  Big tax breaks for humane, regenerative plant protein systems.
- **Cultural detox**
  The real deficiency isn't protein – it's logic, biology, and a few additional moments of focus.

Leaving You With This
(Scientifically irrational, philosophically sound, and politically fortified.)

Crickets aren't the future. They're just crunchy meat with extra limbs. The real protein revolution is quiet, green, currently photosynthesising, and patiently waiting its turn while we debate whether eating a grasshopper is daring, rather than admitting that the solution is already growing.

WTF But True

2023: Europe green-lights crickets for the menu but slaps a gag order on calling plant products 'milk' or 'cheese'.

A policy so nonsensical it almost feels accidental – until you see the lobby money trail lighting up the truth like a town-hall Christmas tree.

Against All Logic

Thailand farms billions of crickets annually mostly for Western export – despite locals traditionally eating far more plants than bugs.

Few things scream 'global progress' louder than shipping insects halfway around the world to replace protein-rich plants already growing locally.

Cricket
(Victima Minima)
Insect species cultivated for human consumption.
Raised, processed, and distributed in large quantities.
Primarily marketed to Western consumers.
The practice is positioned as an alternative protein source.

Frankensnacks

AKA: The Long Goodbye to Slaughter

(Our last attempt to keep chewing on corpses – now with extra science.)

Dumb Scale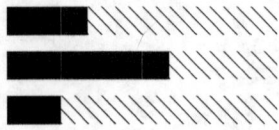
Fixability Index
Outrage Level

The Situation

Humanity finally stared into the moral abyss – and instead of recoiling, someone, inevitably leaned in and whispered, "yeah, yeah, abyss... but can we grill it?"

After centuries of animal sacrifices, barbecues, documentaries and denial, the species collectively threw its hands up and said, "Okay fine, we'll stop killing animals... but can we still eat them? You know – without the screaming part?"

Thus arrived lab-grown meat: the culinary match of mopping the kitchen floor while refusing to turn off the stove. A miracle of modern ethics, stitched together in petri dishes by scientists who quietly wonder when 'please don't eat animals' became a laboratory problem.

The pitch however, is deliciously simple: harvest a few cells, dunk them in a nutrient bath, and grow yourself a guilt-free discount burger. Voila! Flesh without trauma. Meat without murder. Nuggets without nightmares.

But let's not kid ourselves. This isn't a moral transformation – this is guilt delegation, the kind where your conscience clocks out early and leaves a sticky note that says 'handle it yourself, buddy'.

We didn't stop wanting dead flesh; we just needed the blood off *our* hands, so we kept the same guy and changed his coat – from slaughterhouse to lab.

Our kind didn't rise above carnivory – we just rerouted it through stainless steel and hoped nobody would notice.

We are a species so terminally addicted to the taste of its own supremacy, so pathologically attached to the flavour of its own dominance, that when evolution nudged us toward compassion, we created 3D bio-printers and said, "No thanks, we're fine, we'll simulate our own domination instead".

Why It's Ridiculous

Look – lab-grown meat is brilliant science. It's a tectonic upgrade from slaughterhouses. It might save billions of animals, and that deserves champagne, applause, and maybe a parade with confetti made entirely of coconut flakes.

But beneath the innovation lies the punchline: humanity will do anything to avoid personal growth – including inventing an entire industry to simulate the taste of dominion itself.

We could have evolved. We could have said, "You know what, maybe we just stop chewing on tissue fibres that once had a family and a favourite afternoon sunny spot in the field".

But no. Instead, we built chrome terrariums where our denial incubates faster than spores around your dinner plate. Sterile, controlled, carefully detached from the animal it once represented.

It's the ultimate compromise for a species still rooted in the past. We admit it's wrong to kill animals... so we'll just manufacture the product that killing used to produce.

Problem solved! It's ethical theatre. Moral charade, even. A carefully staged performance. A fast-moving game of dodge-ball where accountability never gets called out.

The plant-based equivalent of trying to pee your name in the snow – highly visible, briefly satisfying, and ultimately meaningless.

And the marketing? Oh, it's divine comedy. 'Slaughter-free! Sustainable! Ethical! Progressive!' Sure. So is hummus. But hummus doesn't let you cling to the fantasy that you're still the apex predator at the dinner table.

We're not craving nutrition – we're craving the echos of old power. A reminder that we once ruled by fang and fire, and we're not quite ready to give up that throne.

How to Un-F*ck It

- **Acknowledge the milestone, not the miracle**
  Lab meat may end slaughter – but it won't end the psychology that made slaughter *feel* normal in the first place.
- **Ask the deeper question**
  Are we seeking compassion, or are we just negotiating with it to keep our habits intact?
- **Use it like a bridge, not a shrine**
  Use it to step away from harm. Then keep walking.
- **Let your palate evolve**
  The future doesn't have to taste like a freezer aisle from 1998.
- **And for the love of empathy**
  Stop confusing cleaner hands with cleaner ethics.

Leaving You With This
(Scientifically logical, philosophically illogical, and politically unpopular.)

"I want to be kind – but only if it tastes familiar, is well seasoned, and medium-rare". A dismissive wave of the hand, spoken with a full mouth. This is what compassion looks like once it's filtered through appetite.

Cultured Animal Cells
(Substitutio Carnis)
Biologically engineered, laboratory-grown cellular starter culture.
Designed to replicate the structure and sensory characteristics of meat.
Marketed as a lower-harm alternative to conventional animal products.
Scaled for industrial food production.

The Big Meat Flex

AKA: BBQ Bros

(Steaks, masculinity, and the curious case of nipple tenderness.)

Dumb Scale
Fixability Index
Outrage Level

The Situation

Across the planet, an ancient ritual persists: men gathering around open flames as if reliving a prehistoric meeting where nobody took notes and everybody smelled like decomposing mammoth.

There they stand – chests puffed, brows furrowed, tongs held like sacred relics – clicking them together in a rhythmic chant: *click, click, click*. The ceremonial mating call of the suburban grill master, convinced that reducing once-pink cow flesh to charcoal earns the highest respect of the tribe.

This isn't cooking. It's ritual smoke-signalling performed by adults with the occasional developing black lung.

Generations of ads have drilled one mantra into the male psyche: *Real Men Eat Meat.* Preferably while holding a beer, talking revved engines, and ignoring their recent cholesterol results.

Burger commercials became masculinity boot camps. Steakhouses became temples of testosterone. The barbecue apron evolved into armour, usually stamped with 'Kiss the Cook' (an invitation no one ever acts upon).

Then tofu arrived, quiet, beige, innocent – a neutral and utterly harmless bean product somehow became the villain in a saga of masculine insecurity.

Enter the insult of the century: *Soy Boy*. Nothing rattles a wobbly ego like the threat of plant-based protein.

The mere thought of legumes apparently destabilises the foundations of manhood, built on grill marks, loud engines, and clever marketing.

If tofu can unman you, that masculinity was probably only held together with a splash of barbecue sauce, and sprinkled with a smidgen of denial.

Why It's Ridiculous

Here's the cosmic plot twist: soy *doesn't* give you boobs. Beef might. Yet the oestrogen panic around tofu rages on – a masterclass in internet science: fact-free, meme-powered, and usually shouted by a man whose blood type is gravy.

Phytoestrogens in soy aren't people's oestrogen. They're knock-offs. They fit the human hormonal lock the same way a potato fits a USB port – technically present, functionally useless.

Meanwhile, the hormones in meat and dairy? They're real. Almost identical. And they slot neatly into that lock.

So picture the guy who sneers 'soy boy' while chugging a litre of cow's milk, a substance biologically engineered to turn a 35kg calf into a 400kg adolescent.

He is, in effect, drinking bovine hormones straight from nature's dairy drip while warning others about tofu.

Let that simmer in whatever's left of your critical thinking ability. The 'soy boy' narrative isn't about soy. It's about masculinity trying desperately to feel tall while standing on the shoulders of moo cows.

Ancient heroes feared spears. Modern men fear legumes. Progress...

How to Un-F*ck It

- **Crack open a science book**
  The real kind. Peer-reviewed. Boring as toast and blissfully indifferent to your feelings.
- **Masculinity isn't sold by butchers**
  They're *not* your tribe – they're your saturated-fat suppliers, and they don't care how tough you feel.

- **Worried about oestrogen?**
  If oestrogen worries you, then maybe stop chugging it by the gallon.
- **Understand compassion isn't weakness**
  Real strength doesn't require a victim.
- **Redefine 'manhood' beyond your appetite**
  If spinach scares you, the problem isn't the food.

Leaving You With This
(Scientifically endorsed, philosophically certified, and completely uninvited.)

Now my young boob growers – the true hormonal heavyweight here isn't tofu. It's milk, nature's original muscle potion to turn baby cows into half-tonne wrecking balls.

The irony is planetary: the men shouting "soy makes you feminine!" are guzzling more bovine oestrogen in one milkshake than tofu ever could contain.

Oh, and nature's on the phone. It wants to know why humans keep drinking milk meant for someone else's baby. Go on and try taking a sip from your mum and see how fast that relationship curdles.

BBQ Cooking Tongs
(Instrumentum Potentiae)
Handheld gripping implement.
Used to manipulate animal flesh during cooking.
Frequently framed as an expression of strength, control, or competence.
Meaning is assigned through use.

Hard to Swallow

AKA: SUPPLEMENTS FOR ME, HYPOCRISY FOR THEE

(Why modern diets need supplements – and vegans get blamed.)

Dumb Scale
Fixability Index
Outrage Level

The Situation

Humanity – that proud species who can swallow anti-depressants, daily multivitamins, caffeine pills, vitamin D, fish oil, magnesium gummies shaped like bears – and still uses one B12 tablet as evidence that 'the whole vegan thing just doesn't work'.

Somewhere between breakfast bacon and the third coffee, alarm bells go off:

"VEGANS NEED SUPPLEMENTS!"

Said like it's a scandal. A confession. A nutritional walk of shame.

As if the entire modern food system isn't already being held together by fortification, injections, powders, sprays, pills, and a silent, daily prayer to the vitamin gods.

Let's look at the boringly devastating truth:

The vitamin and supplement industry is worth well over $150 billion globally – and vegans make up a mere 1–3% of the population, depending on the country and how you define 'vegan'.

So unless vegans are single-handedly propping up a multinational industry with nothing but a few small jars of B12 and blind optimism, the math isn't mathing.

The *overwhelming* majority of supplements are bought by omnivores. Daily. Enthusiastically. Often in bulk by the bucket and usually without anyone calling their diet 'incomplete'.

Why It's Ridiculous

The supplement argument pretends there are two separate food systems.

One is "natural". Wholesome. Ancestral. Sun-kissed. A comforting story people tell themselves while eating food shaped by chemistry, fortification, injections, sanitation, and supply chains that circle half the planet.

The other is "artificial". Lab-adjacent. Suspicious. Unfriendly. Identical in every way that matters, except it drops the romance and admits how the nutrients get there.

In reality, there is only one system – and it's been industrialised to hell and back.

Which brings us, inevitably, back to vitamin B12: the poster child of vegan gotchas.

B12 is made by bacteria. Not cows. Not chickens. Not fish. Just single-celled bacteria.

Historically, humans and animals got small amounts from soil, untreated water, and... living much closer to filth and dirt than today.

Modern sanitation cleaned that right out of the picture – along with cholera, typhoid, and most other things that used to kill us before 40.

So what's changed?

Livestock are routinely supplemented with B12. Either directly, or indirectly via cobalt-supplemented feed (cobalt lets *rumen* bacteria make B12). Many animals receive regular injections or fortified feed blends.

In other words:

When someone eats meat for B12, they're not avoiding supplements – they're taking them second-hand. Like borrowing a vitamin that's already been chewed. The cow took the pill. You ate the cow. Great, although you are still supplementing. Same vitamin. Same chemistry. Same dependency. Just with extra steps, saturated fat, and by killing someone who had once a face.

Why You Should Care

This isn't about vitamins. It's about moving the goalposts. When an omnivore supplements, it's 'being proactive about health'. When a vegan supplements, it's 'proof the diet doesn't work'. Same pill. Different narrative.

And here comes the absurdity:
Many omnivorous staple foods are fortified by default.
- Milk with vitamin D
- Breakfast cereals with iron, B vitamins, folate
- Bread and salt with iodine (in many countries)
- Margarine with vitamins A & D

And nobody is screaming **"DIET FAILURE"** at toast.
Now, brace yourself – this is where the ride gets bumpy:

The Great Iodine Plot Twist

Milk is often held up as a 'natural' iodine source. Which is broadly true – but only in the same way traffic noise is a 'natural' part of cities.

The iodine in dairy *isn't* the result of cows thoughtfully producing micronutrients for humans. It's the by-product of an industrial system: feed composition, mineral supplementation, sanitation practices, regional regulations, and historical residue.

Historically, much of the iodine found in milk came not from cows, but from iodine-based disinfectants used to clean dairy equipment.

Modern practices have slightly reduced this – but what remains is still inconsistent and largely accidental, varying wildly by country, season, farm protocol, and the basic care provided by underpaid dairy workers.

In other words, milk doesn't *contain* iodine so much as it actually *acquires* it.

That 'natural iodine' wasn't cultivated with intent. It emerged from a supply chain and stayed because it was convenient.

Meanwhile, an iodine supplement off the shelf is:

- Precisely dosed.
- Consistent.
- Transparent about where the iodine comes from.

No guessing. No seasonal swings. No reliance on agricultural side effects. But sure – let's panic about the humble tablets instead.

How to Un-F*ck It

- Stop pretending supplements are a vegan thing. They're a people thing. Welcome to the 21st century.
- Admit the system is artificial already. The food chain has been fortified, injected, cleaned, sprayed,

scrubbed, dusted and optimised beyond recognition. Nature left this chat decades ago.
- Take the vitamin directly. There!
- Skip the middle-cow. It's more efficient that way and avoids the awkward ethical implications.
- Evaluate diets by what they do, not how they look.

With good health markers, lower-harm delivery methods are ethically preferable.

Leaving You With This
(Clinically simple. Philosophically inconvenient. Socially just wrong.)

The idea that a diet 'fails' because it uses supplements only works if you pretend the rest of the population isn't already swallowing half a pharmacy before lunch.

Vegans didn't invent supplementation. They just removed the animal from the supply chain – and read the label out loud.

WTF But True

The vast majority of global B12 production exists because modern food systems removed natural exposure, not because vegans exist.

Farm animals are commonly supplemented – meaning many people already rely on synthetic vitamins, just filtered through livestock.

The supplement industry would survive perfectly fine if every vegan vanished tomorrow. (Which would be highly unfortunate, but true.)

Against All Logic

Who listens to a man who drinks fortified milk, eats fortified cereal, seasons his food with iodised salt, takes vitamin D in winter – and then points at a vegan's B12 tablet like he's cracked the case?

This isn't just scepticism. It's conscience firing wildly into the wrong crowd.

Vitamin B12
(Cobalamin)
Bacterial-derived micronutrient.
Essential for nerve function and blood formation.
Commonly supplemented across populations.
Disproportionately discussed in counter-vegan debates.

Green Outside, Grilled on the Inside

AKA: Extinction BBQ

(Reusable coffee cups, diesel SUVs and cheeseburger value meals.)

Dumb Scale	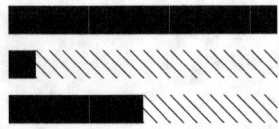
Fixability Index	
Outrage Level	

The Situation

There exists a peculiar breed of eco-warrior roaming the streets with handmade cardboard signs declaring "There Is No Planet B", while sipping a cow's milk latte, polishing off a kebab, and maintaining a careful separation between planetary concern and what's on their plate.

They glue themselves to highways, chain themselves to oil rigs, and lecture strangers about carbon footprints... then swing by the nearest burger joint because activism burns calories and makes you hungry.

Rainforest destruction for beef? Not a peep. Apparently it's only problematic when Shell does it – not when Shelly does it, because then it's "just one burger".

Animal agriculture rivals the emissions of planes, trains, and cars *combined* – and conveniently slips past most climate conversations.

Yet somehow, a mind-boggling number of the eco-crowd still behave as though cows emit their greenhouse gases into another dimension, possibly directly into Narnia.

The folks who refuse plastic straws to save one turtle and then support the industry that bulldozes entire ecosystems.

It's the environmental equivalent of tossing a thimble of water at a burning house, then using the flames to grill a pork shoulder around the back.

Why It's Ridiculous

This kind of mental gymnastics could qualify for the Paralympics. You can't march for the climate while devouring the very thing cooking it. It's like calling the fire brigade and showing up with your own matches – just to be helpful.

You can proudly announce to have 'cut down on red meat', as if cutting down changes reality. Methane doesn't care about your moderation. A moral stance that suspiciously sounds like: "I only stab the planet on weekends".

This flavour of climate activists who eat meat are the flat-earthers of sustainability: loud, confident, and catastrophically missing the point.

Every cheeseburger neutralises a protest sign. Every 'Meatless Monday' cancelled by a Friday night barbecue resets the moral odometer. You see, the laws of thermodynamics are not just opinions.

And yes, before someone says it – no one's perfect. There's imperfection... and then there's delusion wrapped in bacon and butcher's paper.

How to Un-F*ck It

- **Pick a lane**
  Preferably the one not paved with melting ice caps.
- **Rebrand activism into consistency**
  Chanting is easy. Changing lunch takes a bit of will power – and maybe some tempeh.
- **Know your emissions**
  Cows don't sigh carbon dioxide. They're enthusiastically emitting methane at volumes the atmosphere won't forgive us in decades.
- **Stop romanticising 'ethical meat'**
  It's arson-kits in a nice package. It's just a nice box – the fire's the same.

- **Remember why the Amazon burned**
  And no, you cannot offset that with your herb garden out the back. The Amazon wasn't torched for bunches of mint and basil.
- **Real activism starts at the dinner table**
  It demands more than slogans, signs, or a weekend protest.

Leaving You With This
(Scientifically strange, philosophically sound, and socially questionable.)

And yes – patience, my young Padawans – this one's aimed at veterinarians, wildlife carers, zookeepers, and rehabbers too – you shall not be spared.

Noble hearts, incredible people... but maybe stop bottle-feeding an orphaned joey at noon and slow-cooking someone else's baby at six. The hypocrisy writes itself; the lamb, tragically, is already silenced. Hard to preach compassion when dinner still has a family tree.

And if Greta Thunberg wanted to end emissions overnight, she wouldn't need another UN speech. Just a big **'CLOSED FOR RENOVATIONS'** sign on every butcher shop around the world.

Promotional Tote Bag
(Ethica Superficialis)
Reusable carry bag printed with commercial fast-food branding.
Produced as part of a sustainability-focused marketing initiative.
Associates environmental messaging with animal-based food products.
Distributed for consumer use.

Bro-Science: In Protein We Trust

AKA: Where Do You Get Your Bro-tein?

(How the humble amino acid made us keep chewing on the dead.)

Dumb Scale	
Fixability Index	
Outrage Level	

The Situation

At some point in recent history – scholars disagree if it was sometime between the rise of gym culture and the moment someone decided vitamins should taste like lollies – protein became humanity's favourite cult.

Forget "Hello". Forget "How are you?" The modern greeting is: "But bro... where do you get your protein?"

It's become the sacred riddle of the gym temple, whispered with the seriousness of a monk guarding ancient scrolls.

Never mind that the average protein expert can't define a single amino acid. Their faith is absolute; their knowledge about it, is completely – absent.

The myth is absurdly simple: 'stop eating animals and your muscles will vanish overnight'.

The truth, of course, is that animals don't manufacture protein from scratch. They steal it from plants. Those sneaky little critters!

It's second-hand protein – pre-chewed gains, so to speak. And so the logic goes like this: Cow eats plants, builds muscle. Human eats cow and decides protein comes from cow.

That's basic biology.

Calling the cow the *source* is the mistake. Remove the cow and nothing breaks.

Why It's Ridiculous

Let's start with the basics, so listen up Gymbro!

Protein is made of amino acids – nine of which your body can't make. These are found in almost every whole food on Earth. Yes, even broccoli. Even oats and definitely that lentil you flicked off your plate last Sunday.

But the meat lobby turned 'complete protein' into a holy grail – as if everyday protein-rich meals were something rare and elusive.

They made protein sound exclusive – like there's a secret amino acid that only appears after passing through animal flesh.

Marketing did the rest. Now we have:
- Protein bars
- Protein cookies
- Protein cereal
- Protein water
- Protein beer (yes, this is a *real* product)

At this point, I'm surprised we don't have Protein Toothpaste – for the extra bulking while brushing.

If it can be swallowed, someone's added '*protein*' to it and doubled the price. And still, no one corners the meat-eater with the far more urgent question: "Mate, where do you get your fibre?"

Why You Should Care

Protein deficiency is the Loch Ness Monster of Western nutrition – endlessly discussed, rarely spotted.

In the developed world, it's virtually nonexistent; instead, we choose a lack of fresh fruit, vegetables, and above all, common sense.

This obsession props up entire industries, funding billion-dollar supplement companies.

- It keeps people eating corpses for fear their abs will shrink overnight.

- Supplement companies rake in fortunes selling powdered hope in buckets the size of toddlers.
- Influencers pose with shaker bottles like their authority arrives premixed.

Meanwhile, elephants, rhinos, horses, and gorillas, nature's original herbivorous demolition crew, are out there living their best lives, quietly proving that plants build more muscle than any marketing department ever has.

But sure, tell the vegan they're weak, wheezing up a flight of stairs while your Fitbit reminds you to breathe.

How to Un-F*ck It

- **National Renaming Campaign**
  Rename 'protein' to 'amino acid confetti' – and observe an instant drop in macho energy.
- **Introduce the 'Bro-tein Tax™'**
  A compulsory $2 surcharge plus a mandatory salad for anyone using gym-jargon by saying "gains" or "do you even lift" in public.
- **Mandatory reading**
  Teach children that peas contain protein before advertising propaganda ruins their minds.
- **New labelling reform**
  Products must disclose their protein *source*, e.g.

- **Chicken Breast** – reassembled plant protein, routed through a bird, for reasons nobody can quite justify anymore.
- **Whey Powder** – dried up cow's milk residue plus a crap-load of really clever marketing.
- **Black Beans** – just protein – really.
- **Launch a reality show**
  The Great Protein Hunt – contestants search desperately for protein while surrounded by it.

Leaving You With This
(Scientifically hot, philosophically cold, and socially lukewarm at best.)

If protein improved comprehension as reliably as it boosts confidence, this chapter wouldn't have been necessary.

Instead, we are online debating whether legumes possess mysterious properties and if tofu reduces testosterone through some mystical ju-ju energy, unknown to modern science.

WTF But True

The average adult needs roughly 0.8 grams of protein per kilogram of body weight per day – easily met by eating plants, grains, legumes, or basically anything that once photosynthesised.

Unless you live in the USA, where the latest food pyramid suggests 1.2–1.6g per kilogram – presumably after a long complimentary lunch hosted by its sponsors.

Finally we are bringing young Brandon from the mail room in line with bodybuilders and athletes burning through thousands of calories per day.

Yet most gym-going mortals consume *double* that amount. Not because their muscles need it – but because protein powder companies do.

The protein supplement industry? Over $20 billion a year. A monument to the fact that we don't lack protein – we lack understanding and basic scientific comprehension.

Against All Logic

When asked about vegan diets, one bodybuilder once famously declared,
"Plants don't have enough protein to build muscle".

Remarkable confidence in cholesterol-clown logic, eating plant protein with extra steps and a corpse in the middle.

Protein Powder Scoop
(Mensura Fidei)
Injection-moulded plastic utensil.
Used to portion powdered protein supplements for human consumption.
Designed to standardise intake beyond recommended dietary sources.
Often associated with contemporary fitness and supplementation practices.

Buzz Buzz Buzz

AKA: TURNING POLLINATORS INTO SUGAR SLAVES

(Bees, honey, and the routine of stealing lunch from the workforce.)

Dumb Scale
Fixability Index
Outrage Level

The Situation

Meet the humble bee – pollinating the world. Quietly. Efficiently. Unnoticed.

They do it so well that roughly a third of human food depends on them – fruits, vegetables, nuts, seeds – the kind of essentials the average person assumes will always be there.

And humanity looked at this miracle of ecological cooperation and thought: "Fantastic. Let's put it in a box. Monetise it. Then skim the profits from selling the bee vomit".

Enter the honey industry – where a wild insect becomes a managed commodity, a hive becomes livestock, and a teaspoon of sweetness requires industrial logistics, smoke machines, trucks, chemicals, and a surprising amount of denial.

Why It's Ridiculous

Let's start with the star employee: the European honey bee (*Apis mellifera*). Not native to most of the places it's now trucked through like a touring boy band. Not particularly good at pollinating native plants either. In fact – compared to many native bees – it's objectively bad at it.

Honey bees are generalists. Native bees are specialists. Generalists dabble. Specialists get the job done.

Yet we flood ecosystems with honey bees anyway, because they're easy to manage, easy to exploit, and excellent at producing something humans insist they need despite surviving just fine for 99.99% of their evolutionary history without squeezing it out of insects.

Queens are often artificially inseminated and glued to the base of the hive. The hives themselves are chemically managed. Wings are clipped and entire colonies are killed when inconvenient.[2]

And in colder climates? Hives are often burned over winter – a much cheaper option than keeping them alive. Other times, the bees are left alive but fed sugar water instead... because the honey they made for themselves was already taken and dripped on your half burnt breakfast toast this morning.

Imagine working all summer, storing food for winter, then having your pantry stripped bare and replaced

---

2 Animal welfare is our top priority.

with jars of nutrient-empty sugar sludge that keeps you alive, not well – just alive.

Now imagine acting surprised when disease spreads.

How Something So Sweet Got So Wrong

The story sold to humans is wholesome. Gentle. Almost Disney. Happy bees. Golden fields. Gentle buzzing. A soft-handed beekeeper humming while stealing the emergency rations of an entire colony.

Reality is less storybook, more logistics chain. Commercial beekeeping involves transporting hives across countries to service mono-culture crops – almonds, blueberries, apples – creating stress, immune suppression, and ideal conditions for parasites like the *Varroa mite* to thrive.

Those diseases don't politely stay put. They spill into wild populations, infecting native bees with no exposure, no resistance, and no protection.

Result:

- Native bee decline
- Reduced pollination efficiency
- Less biodiversity
- More ecological fragility

All so humans can drizzle something gooey on their crackers and call it 'natural sweetener'.

Why You Should Care

Because bees aren't interchangeable widgets. And pollination isn't a task you can scale infinitely without consequences.

Native bees pollinate more effectively than honey bees – some by vibrating flowers (a skill honey bees lack entirely), others by timing their life cycles perfectly with local plants.

- When honey bees dominate, native bees lose food, space, and health.
- When native bees disappear, ecosystems unravel – devastatingly.
- And when ecosystems unravel, humans panic – then invent solutions and sell them back to themselves.

And yes – before anyone asks – honey bees have a central nervous system and a teeny-tiny brain with around a million neurons. They learn. They remember. They even communicate locations, threats, and resources through interpretive dance.

They are not just generous sugar fairies.

How to Un-F*ck It

- Stop pretending honey is essential. It isn't. Sugar exists. So does maple syrup, date syrup, agave, rice malt, fruit – and, in rare cases, basic self-control.
- Support habitat restoration for native bees, not the mass placement of managed hives into already stressed landscapes.
- Shift agriculture away from mono-cultures that require constant pollination support.
- Regulate commercial beekeeping as an ecological intervention, not a cottage hobby.
- Teach kids that "saving the bees" doesn't mean farming them – it means leaving space for wild ones to exist.

Leaving You With This
(Scientifically grounded, philosophically irritating, and entirely deserved.)

If an animal makes food to survive winter and you take it because it tastes nice, you are not harvesting. You are looting. Calling it 'ethical honey' doesn't change the math. It just sweetens the story while everything else pays for it.

WTF But True

Almond milk is often criticised for bee exploitation – yet the honey industry runs on the same mass hive transport system, exporting parasites and diseases across continents.

The bees work harder so humans can keep arguing about ethics while sweetening their tea with stolen insect calories.

Against All Odds

Urban wildflower corridors, pesticide bans, and native-bee conservation projects are quietly working. When honey bees stop being the headline act, ecosystems start recovering.

Turns out when you stop farming pollinators and start protecting them, nature does most of the heavy lifting for free.

Honey Spoon
(Extractio Dulcis)
Utensil designed for the collection and transfer of honey.
Used in food preparation and consumption.
Associated with sweetening practices in human diets.
Linked to managed apiculture systems.

The Lion Made Me Do It

AKA: Lions Tho! They Eat Gazelles, Bro

(Notes from the apex predator who hasn't stood up from the couch in days.)

Dumb Scale
Fixability Index
Outrage Level

The Situation

There's a certain kind of armchair philosopher – usually spotted near barbecues, gyms, or a Nintendo controller, basically any location where conversation and waistlines collide – who believes he has discovered the ultimate vegan-smashing argument.

He leans in, drops his voice, and delivers his thesis like a knock-off Attenborough who believes whispering alone makes him educated: "Lions eat gazelles, bro".

And there it is – the 'Circle of Life' Card, slammed down with the confidence of someone who thinks watching one nature documentary once is comparable to finishing a degree in predatory ethics.

The logic – simple enough to fit on the back of a beer coaster: lions eat meat, humans are animals too, therefore humans eating meat is natural. Case closed.

Except that by this reasoning, so is sniffing your boss's butt in the morning (not entirely unheard of), drowning rival offspring in the water cooler, and licking yourself clean in the middle of a shopping aisle.

Nature isn't a moral guidebook – it's a chaotic shitshow of hunger, desperation, and animals doing whatever it takes not to become lunch today.

The lion doesn't pause for ethical debate. It doesn't weigh the moral implications of a gazelle screaming versus that same gazelle running. The lion operates on instinct. Humans, supposedly, don't.

The whole 'nature' argument is the culinary equivalent of saying "my dog eats poo, so humans should too".

A lion kills because it *must*. You order a cheeseburger because it pairs well with large fries and apathy.

The moment someone compares their dinner to a wildlife documentary, you need to listen *very* closely – because you can actually hear their moral conscience flipping the main light switch off – all the way on the back wall and going to bed early.

Why It's Ridiculous

Let's pull the thread. The lion eats gazelles because it can't invent agriculture, use a fork, or learn how to bake sourdough during lock-down. You, on the other hand, live in a world where chickpeas are cheap and your fridge has an internet connection.

The lion doesn't apply for subsidies to industrialise suffering. It doesn't breed gazelles by the billions, cage them, force-feed them, or market a new 'Savannah-Prime™ Rib-eye Experience' with a limited-time dipping sauce.

It kills the old-fashioned way: claws, teeth, hunger, and zero interest in turning misery into a brand name.

Humans kill with efficiency, pipelines, machinery and ethics so abstracted they arrive with batch numbers.

If you truly want to follow nature's lead, you'd also need to start eating your meat raw, sleeping under bushes, lapping from muddy puddles, and marking your territory wherever the urge strikes, even if that means behind your annoying neighbour's SUV.

Suddenly the "we're natural predators" routine gets quite real – real fast. Morality seems to return the moment personal hygiene is on the line – and suddenly becomes as uncomfortable as a splinter under your nail.

Quoting lions to justify lunch is like using toddlers to justify your own tantrums. Nature is not an instruction manual. It's a warning label. Our current civilisation exists for a reason: we *don't* use animal behaviour to ethically validate our own actions.

How to Un-F*ck It

- **Stop outsourcing ethics to wildlife**
  Lions don't provide moral guidance. They provide survival strategies – and you are not one of them. *(Looking at you Ryan.)*
- **Remember evolution**
  We didn't evolve bigger brains and empathy just to build larger barbecues. We also evolved them to question *what* we put on the grill.
- **Distinguish 'can' from 'should'**
  Humanity can split atoms, clone sheep, and deep-fry pretty much anything. None of that tells us what we *ought* to do.
- **Study the lion properly**
  It kills only when hungry – never for flavour, and never because it felt peckish during binge night.
- **Realise morality begins where instinct ends**
  If instinct is your compass, don't be surprised when it leads you in circles – excellent for survival, less so for ethics.

Leaving You With This
(Scientifically valid, philosophically strange, and socially unacceptable.)

If 'natural' automatically meant 'good', we'd all be hoping to bring back smallpox, open sewers, and the possibility of dying at thirty-two because a minor cut got infected before antibiotics existed.

Nature isn't a *moral* guide. It's a very effective teacher with no interest in your comfort or well-being and our civilisation exists precisely because we decided to listen to that teacher.

Camouflage Baseball Cap
(Predator Imaginarius)
Patterned headwear designed to mimic natural environments.
Associated with hunting, outdoor, and wildlife-related activities.
Often used in contexts referencing survival or natural hierarchy.
Linked to cultural narratives of human alignment with apex predators.

Pampered Prisoners

AKA: I Love You. (That's Why I've Put You in A Cage)

(Our obsession with owning pets.)

Dumb Scale
Fixability Index
Outrage Level

The Situation

Humans love animals. Especially the furry ones. Naturally, the first step is to breed them, use them, and sell them to other humans.

We name them; put bows on their heads and chips in their necks. We feed them processed meat in shapes nature never intended; trap them in apartments and reassure them: "You're part of the family now".

Adorable – although in this family, 'belonging' means wearing a flea collar and pooping in a plastic tub filled with lemon-scented gravel.

Common Domestication Dynamics:
- **Cats**
  Brought indoors, neutered, and laser-pointed into every-other-night confusion.

- **Dogs**
  Bred for aesthetics, then left home alone for nine hours with a squeaky chicken and a Wi-Fi nanny-cam documenting the aftermath of who pooped in the kitchen.
- **Birds**
  Flight-capable beings locked in decorative cages so we can enjoy their songs from exactly 45 centimetres away, occasionally whistling back at them. 'Freedom' is now a mirror and a human index finger pointing at them.
- **Snakes & Lizards**
  Kidnapped from their natural ecosystems, and relocated to a suburban glass box with an overhead heat lamp. Renamed 'Kevin', and fed thawed rodents every second Thursday.
- **Fish**
  Water-bound ornaments circling the same eight litres of milky water indefinitely, guarding their LED-lit plastic castle relentlessly, like tiny, unblinking prisoners.
- **Horses**
  Majestic creatures, born to roam plains; now kept in paddocks wearing glitter strings in their braided mane, used on Saturdays by young adults who call themselves 'horse girls'.

Why It's Ridiculous

Domestication traded instinct for dependency. We build a world where dogs unravel when left alone, parrots scream in suburban kitchens for 50 years straight, and entire species vanish unnoticed because they weren't cute enough to be collared, caged, or sold into confinement for our comfort.

Why You Should Care

'Love' quietly becomes ownership. We don't have companions – we have emotionally dependent roommates we dress up as elves when December rolls around.

Domestication didn't make them family. It made them decoratively compliant tenants whose rent is obedience and whose freedoms exist entirely at our convenience.

We may call it 'affection', but it's really just Stockholm Syndrome with some treats. Calling a dog a 'family member' sounds wholesome... until you notice most family members aren't kept on scheduled toilet intervals or rewarded with treats for correctly performing a trick or displaying obedience on command.

What we label as 'care' is often just control with unwanted cuddles and confinement when convenient.

How to Un-F*ck It

- **Pet role reversal day**
  One day a year, humans wear the leash, eat dry pellets, poop in a box and must sit politely before being allowed outside. Treats may be earned by solving basic enrichment puzzles.
- **Freedom rating labels**
  Every pet sold comes with a 'Freedom Score', ranging from *Lives Like Royalty* to *Decorative Prisoner*.
- ***'It's Not You, It's Zoo'* education campaign**
  Public messaging reminding people that just because an animal can't ask for help, doesn't mean it doesn't need it.
- **Affection time audits**
  Track the actual hours spent with your beloved 'fur baby'. Less than four hours per week suggests captivity. Full ownership is complete when your affection correlates directly with how little they resist being occasionally dressed like a taco.

Leaving You With This
(Philosophically disgruntled, ethically itchy, and generally not needed.)

Love shouldn't require a cage. Not even that pastel-pink one with the cute water bottle and the engraved food dish reading ♥ Toby ♥

WTF But True

Parrots in captivity often pluck out every feather they have. We call it 'quirky'. It's not. It's the avian equivalent of a 50-year daily panic attack performed in front of a mirror.

Pet turtles can live 40, 50, even 60 years. Meaning 'that cute little gift for the kids' will outlast the kids' childhood, your marriage, your second marriage, your mortgage, and occasionally your will to scrub the algae from the tank.

Against All Odds

In the Netherlands, some animal shelters now require human–animal compatibility interviews. Think Tinder for dogs – but with fewer red flags, better screening, and a far higher success rate.

Identification Microchip Implant *(Enlarged scale model)*
(Proprietas Interna)
Implantable electronic identification device.
Used to assign permanent ownership and traceability.
Applied within domestic animal management systems.

Death Sticks & Dad Jokes

AKA: STABBING ANIMALS WITH DAD

(A father–son bonding activity involving animal torture.)

Dumb Scale
Fixability Index
Outrage Level

The Situation

Initially, fishing sounds peaceful: gentle rivers, quiet mornings, bird-songs, sunrise glistening over the water. In reality, it's blood sport conducted with a picnic basket and a six-pack.

Humans call it 'recreation', but the fish call it 'Tuesday'.

It's a well-established form of stress relief: stabbing strangers with metal hooks and watching them suffocate – the human version of spearing a random passer-by to unwind after a long day's work.

Nothing says 'quality time with Dad' like impaling a sentient creature with a hook while casually discussing last weekend's footy scores.

Ask any fisherman and he'll puff out his chest and say, "Fish don't feel pain". Which is quite clearly and scientifically inaccurate but emotionally rather convenient – it is also part of the same reasoning that once declared whales 'resources' and forests 'infinite'.

Fish *absolutely* feel pain. They have *nociceptors* – pain receptors. They exhibit stress responses. They form memories. Some can even recognise human faces, which means they likely recognise the one yanking them into the sky.

All fun facts that makes the whole 'catch of the day' routine feel less like sport and more like a hit-men get-together.

But the hairless ape adores this ritual. A wholesome pastime! A rite of passage! A spiritual retreat where you murder something slowly enough to still notice how pretty the scenery is while telling your kid not to cry.

And if fishing is too subtle for you, we invented 'catch and release', the moral equivalent of waterboarding a stranger then saying, "Don't worry mate – I'll let him go after I'm done with him". You might as well be roughing someone up in a back alley, then saying it's fine because you didn't keep their wallet.

Why It's Ridiculous

Here comes the cosmic punchline – though the joke stops being funny: fishing is the only activity where people intentionally torture animals *and* high-five themselves for being patient while doing it.

Imagine if other hobbies worked like this:
- **Knitting**
  Every third stitch, and someone gets stabbed in the eye.
- **Yoga**
  The instructor quietly chokes someone between poses for 'alignment'.
- **Golf**
  The club doesn't touch the ball – but the guy next to you gets it in chest.

The absurdity is staggering. Humanity claims to love oceans, cherish marine life, and protect the environment – then promptly heads out to skewer the inhabitants – to kill them and some time before Sunday lunch.

And let's not forget to address the cultural mythology: 'Fishing teaches discipline!' So does meditation. So does mowing the lawn. So does *not* sticking sharp objects into living things.

Yet society treats this like wholesome bonding – as if the emotional cornerstone of fatherhood involves killing helpless animals together on weekends.

Christianity has the Holy Trinity. Fishing families have the Unholy Trinity: Insulated cooler, murder sticks, and generational numbness.

And all of this is justified because fish 'look different'. They don't scream. They don't bleed red. They don't make the sad Pixar eyes. They just look back at you with that blank expression that lets humans pretend nothing's happening. They just gasp in panic until they silently die.

How to Un-F*ck It

- **Acknowledge the obvious**
  Ending a life 'to relax' or for fun is *not* cool.
- **Retire the 'fish don't feel pain' myth**
  If you're going to end a life, at least have the decency not to lie about it.
- **Bond over something else**
  Maybe share a fruit-cup or throw a Frisbee with your kid instead of a hook into someone's face.
- **Respect the ecosystem by not harpooning it**
  A radical idea, apparently, for creatures who invented the harpoons.
- **Try ocean activities where nothing dies**
  Kayaking. Swimming. Paddle-boarding. Zero victims. Everyone goes home happy.

- **Examine why 'relaxation' requires bloodshed**
  Therapy is cheaper than a boat and doesn't involve flinging polished, high-carbon steel hooks into marine life that was having a perfectly fine day before you came along.

Leaving You With This
(Scientifically iced, philosophically melted, and socially sticky.)

'Catch-and-release' is the only sport where torture followed by release counts as compassion. Apply that logic elsewhere and see how that goes.

Fishing Hook
(Instrumentum Penetrationis)
Sharpened steel alloy component attached to a tensioned line.
Designed to pierce the soft tissue of aquatic animals.
Configured to maintain restraint during extraction from water.
Widely used in commercial and recreational fishing.

Meat Prescription

AKA: DOCTOR, I GET DIZZY WITHOUT BACON

(Diagnosing a deficiency that doesn't exist.)

Dumb Scale
Fixability Index
Outrage Level

The Situation

Somewhere between the rise of TikTok wellness and the mass extinction of human attention spans, a peculiar sickness began sweeping through a very specific corner of the internet:

The 'Carnivore Condition' – a self-diagnosed affliction where the human body allegedly enters a full system shutdown unless slapped repeatedly with steaks and beef jerky every four hours or so.

No one knows the patient zero. Some suspect it was born in a gym changing room under fluorescent lighting and the faint smell of protein farts. Others trace it to an influencer who once ate a salad, felt a single human emotion, panicked, and immediately blamed the delicate lettuce.

The tale always hits the same beats:

"I tried going vegan for a few hours, and suddenly I lost all energy, my hair fell out, my toenails curled up, and my dog stopped respecting me. My doctor said I have to eat steak – he ran no tests but assured me it's genetic".

Then, inevitably: steakhouse selfie. Caption: *Healing.*

Meanwhile, their body continues doing exactly what bodies do – all vital systems remain operational.

This isn't medicine. It's nutritional ignorance. The modern sequel to hypochondria, but with more hashtags and fewer working brain cells. It's the WebMD of caveman fantasies – loud, confident, and medically illiterate.

They gnaw raw liver on camera, warning the world that broccoli is definitely toxic to them.

Meanwhile Darwin, down in his eternal resting place, is clawing at the inside of his coffin lid, muttering, "You people cannot be serious".

Why It's Ridiculous

Let's start with the easy bit: there's *no* known medical condition that requires slaughtering animals, stripping them of their flesh and eating it to stay alive. Unless you count capitalism, which does rely on turning living things into products – but that's a different conversation.

The human digestive system didn't crawl out of the evolutionary soup just to crumble upon contact with a chickpea.

We're omnivores by option, not obligation. It's a built-in feature, meaning we *can* eat meat, not that we'll collapse without it. But try telling that to the guy holding a rib-eye like it's an EpiPen.

These are the same warriors of 'ancestral living' who shout 'nature intended!' while sitting in a synthetic recliner engineered by a company in South East Asia older than their keto fantasies.

Their logic is at performance level and it goes like this:
- **Step 1:** "Plants make me bloated".
- **Step 2:** "Therefore plants are bad".
- **Step 3:** "Therefore steak is medicine".

"Bam! There I told you – you crazy vegoons! Steak is medicine".

By that logic, if running makes you tired, sleep must be exercise.

If broccoli is considered toxic, the issue isn't nutrition – it's basic logic.

How to Un-F*ck It

- **Log out of influencer-land**
  If someone tries to sell desiccated beef organs with discount codes, maybe don't take medical advice from them. Just a thought.
- **Consult a real doctor**
  Preferably one with a degree, not an Etsy store and a one day internet course on the subject of nutritional science.
- **If plants *genuinely* upset your stomach**
  See an *actual* nutritionist before announcing that spinach is teaming up with Big-Pharma.

Also – and this part's crucial – consider that maybe, just maybe, what people mistake for 'missing meat' is usually salt, fat, artificial flavour, the occasionally stern talking-to from their mother or perhaps the warm illusion of belonging to a gym tribe that high-fives each other after dead-lifts.

Leaving You With This
(Scientifically outdated, philosophically timeless, and fashionably late.)

If 'meat deficiency' were a real disease, hospitals would have entire emergency wings devoted to steak transfusions. The absence of such wards is... telling.

Medical Dictionary
(Necessitas Assumpta)
Reference documenting recognised diseases, conditions, and treatments.
Used to standardise medical terminology and clinical knowledge.
Contains no established condition requiring animal flesh.
Consulted in clinical and academic settings.

Planet of the Caged

AKA: Cages With Gift Shops

(How we lock up wildlife, call it 'care', and sell tickets to the circus.)

Dumb Scale
Fixability Index
Outrage Level

The Situation

We lock wild animals in oversized cabinets and call it 'education', as if a giraffe pacing a perfect concrete oval teaches anyone anything – except the vague, nagging sense that something here is feeling deeply off.

Then we slap the word 'conservation' on the gate, sell $12 buckets of hot chips that taste like wet cardboard, and let toddlers point at lions staring motionless past the fence-lines.

Meanwhile the parents chomp on Pluto pups while the kids pet piglets, lambs and baby goats a few metres away – the same species the signs claims we're 'saving'. The irony could power a small city.

Marine parks? No problem – roofie the dolphins until they're compliant enough to flip on cue and watch the audience clap like well-trained, obedient seals.

And then – let's not forget – there are the racetracks. Industries churning through horses and dogs like gamblers burning through paychecks. Whenever an animal collapses, they're quietly swept aside and swapped out like a faulty Kmart toaster.

Which finally brings us to the labs, sealed off with an *impressive* commitment to privacy. Primates strapped into medieval contraptions so researchers can keep repeating experiments older than your Nan's wall clock.

Then, as we exit through the gift shop and re-enter the spectacle: we are instructed to parrot after the tour guide: "That polar bear doing laps in his blue plastic Arctic pool is *definitely* happier here".

Why It's Ridiculous

- **Zoos**

    A conservation story where the animals are captured and confined. They circle, sway, stare into the middle distance, and unravel in slow motion over many years. The only thing being conserved is ticket revenue.[3]

- **Racing**

    An industry that treats living beings as potentially faulty inventory. If the body stops performing, it's

---

3   Animal welfare is our top priority.

written off, cleared away, replaced, and turned into pet food or fertiliser before the punters finish chewing their $14 bacon sandwich.

- **Lab experiments**

    Decades-old tests regurgitated out of habit, not discovery. Primates strapped to machinery so someone can confirm a finding carved into scientific stone generations ago. This is not research anymore; it's just bureaucracy without a heartbeat.

- **Sanctuaries that breed**

    The moral rebrand where cages are painted in soothing colours and the brochure screams 'care'. Breeding programs wrapped in soft lighting and buzzwords, turning baby animals into fundraising props. Sanctuary in name, a zoo in practice.

Collectively, these industries don't solve problems; they *preserve* them – and charge a small admission fee.

Why You Should Care

Captive animals don't get 'bored'. They disintegrate from the inside out: pacing tight loops, rocking from left to right to nowhere, grinding their teeth on metal bars until something gives – usually them.

Those cheerful zoo photos? Mugshots, professionally lit, photo-shopped and tastefully branded.

Racing industries overbreed, confine, injure, dope and discard horses and greyhounds on repeat. Grief is brief. Administration is thorough. Public statements confirm the animals were 'loved', 'valued', and 'well cared for', phrases usually reserved for things that have already been discarded.

Millions of lab animals endure experiments with questionable relevance and unrelated to human biology. The practice still persists, if only out of habit.

Kids learn early that a cage equals care. Domination doesn't arrive loudly – it shows up polite, laminated, and labelled 'Education'.

The damage isn't just to animals. It's to the very definition of human compassion.

How to Un-F*ck It

- **Ban the supply chain**
  Cut off the pipeline. No breeding, trading, or capturing wildlife for entertainment, education, or the illusion of good parenting on a Sunday afternoon zoo visit.
- **Shut it down**
  Commence the gradual decommissioning and repurposing of zoos, marine parks, and racetracks – all remaining captivity infrastructure.

Turn the space into real sanctuaries or restore it to actual habitat – places where animals can behave like themselves, not perform for coupons.

- **Modernise science**

  Where non-animal methods exist – and they do – animal testing belongs in the archive. Time to update legislation written in the rotary-phone era.

- **Upgrade education**

  Replace school trips to Animal Prison-Land™ with immersive digital safaris, live wildlife cams, and science labs that teach biology without the casualties.

- **No more exploitation sports**

  If speed is the goal, ride a bike or sprint yourself. There's a perfectly good footpath nearby. No animal participation required.

None of this is complicated. All of this is just – choice.

Leaving You With This
(Scientifically examined, philosophically explored, and utterly uncalled for.)

Captivity calls itself conservation. Experimentation rebrands as innovation. Entertainment assures us it's justified. Not one of them is telling the truth.

If we insist on calling ourselves the advanced species, then maybe it's time to close the tents on the world's longest, bleakest circus where the animals are dying to entertain us, and let the performers finally go home.

We've had centuries to get this right. It's time to move on.

WTF But True

The vast majority of drugs that pass animal tests still fail in humans. Millions of animals later, the conclusion remains unchanged: we are not mice, dogs, or primates. Biology seems to have grasped this well ahead of our regulations.

Against All Odds

Lab Rats Retire: In 2022, the FDA Modernisation Act opened the door to non-animal testing for drug approval. It took decades of evidence, pressure, and persistence. Progress, apparently, prefers a slow crawl.

Steel Panel Section
(Containmentum Permanente)
*Structural component used in animal containment systems.
Restricts animal movement beyond designated boundaries
for display or management purposes.
Surface wear is consistent with repeated animal interaction.*

Smoke Gets in Your Skies

AKA: BURNING FORESTS, SERVED MEDIUM-RARE

(Turning habitat into calories, briefly.)

Dumb Scale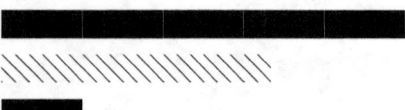
Fixability Index
Outrage Level

The Situation

Animal agriculture isn't a food system. It's a destruction engine with greasy fingerprint smudges all over the crime scene.

Behind the Sunday roast and the cheerful BBQ ad – you know, the one where a smiling family man flips carcinogens, certain this is what 'good people do' – lurks your planetary killer:

- ~80% of global farmland swallowed by livestock and their feed.
- 15–20% of all greenhouse gases, a planetary fart joke without the punchline.
- Forests carved up for animal feed, with discounted flat-pack furniture hitching the ride.
- Oceans stripped of life like someone rage-cleaned them on a Sunday morning.
- Antibiotic resistance, built into the system.

- Pandemic roulette – spin the wheel, participation mandatory, everyone plays, nobody wins.

And the real-head scratcher: we feed perfectly good human food to animals so humans *can't* eat it. The excuses? Taste. Tradition. Protein panic. Lobby money. All of which collapse the moment they're poked with a recyclable plastic fork, coated with a smidgen of science and common sense.

Why It's Ridiculous

Over 80% of the world's soy goes straight into animals, not people – while 800 million humans go hungry and the planet sweats like a sauna with a broken thermostat.

Seventy-plus billion land animals and *trillions* of fish are killed every year and global hunger remains. Apparently, that wasn't the fix.

We're literally torching forests so someone can keep their 'cheat day' bacon sandwich – an uncomfortable truth with a side of ashes and a body count.

But the clever mammal shrugs because it's 'normal'. Repeat a catastrophe long enough and it becomes ingrained culture.

Why You Should Care

- **Climate chaos**

  Methane and CO_2 emissions rivalling entire industrial sectors.

- **Land gluttony**

  Forests cleared not to feed people, but to feed animals first.

- **Health fallout**

  Preventable chronic diseases clogging arteries and hospitals alike.

- **Moral blind spot**

  Industrial slaughter rebranded as 'humane' – the ethical equivalent of slapping a smiley face sticker on a guillotine.

This isn't just bad ethics. It's bad math, bad policy, and a spectacularly reckless way to treat the only planet we have access to without a spacesuit.

How to Un-F*ck It

- **Global plant-based transition**

  No longer a diet trend – it's our new survival strategy – the one we keep pretending is personal choice.

- **Phase out subsidies**
  Stop spending billions propping up destructive industries long past their usefulness. Redirect the money to oats, hemp, mushrooms, seaweed – actual food with a future.
- **Mandatory product climate labelling**
  e.g. *'May contribute to deforestation, climate instability, antibiotic resistance, and very uncomfortable questions from people not even born yet'.*
- **Universal plant-based school meals**
  Let kids inherit health, not heart disease. Let them inherit forests, not feedlots.
- **Rewilding**
  Stop feeding soy to pigs and entire continents get their lungs back – ecologically and biologically (including ours).

The Farmer Factor

This isn't a war on farmers. It's phase one of a planetary emergency rescue mission.

Most livestock farmers are trapped in debt, squeezed by corporations, doing work they never planned but inherited along with the mortgage.

Give them buyouts instead of subsidising their destructive actions, provide retraining, and the infrastructure to grow climate-proof food. Nobody's being tossed off the bus – we're just changing the route before it hits the wall.

Leaving You With This
(Scientifically approved, philosophically irritating, and entirely unrequested.)

Participating in killing for pleasure was never a 'personal choice'. It doubles as a collective suicide note, handwritten in burger grease.

WTF But True

The world raises 70+ billion land animals every year – yet 800 million humans still go hungry.

Apparently feeding corn to chickens is more urgent than feeding it to children.

If cows were a country, they'd rank as the third-largest greenhouse gas-emitter on the planet – right behind China and the US, and well ahead of "Oops, we didn't think this one through".

Against All Odds

Farmer Flip: Pilot programs in the UK and US are paying livestock farmers to switch to oats, re-wilding land, or renewable energy projects – basically anything except another cow.

Farmers are now being paid *not* to farm animals – a very quiet admission that the old model was never viable, just subsidised.

The Decade of Decline:

Global meat consumption per capita has peaked. Germany, the UK – even parts of Australia – are eating less meat without riots, shortages, or civilisation collapsing into tofu-fuelled anarchy.

So much for the apocalypse.

Meat Patty *(Plasticised)*
(Carcinogen Acceptus)
Multi-animal-derived food product. Formed for ease of handling.
Classified as carcinogenic by international health authorities.
Linked in environmental assessments to
high greenhouse gas emissions and resource use.

Gambling on Legs

AKA: FUN WAYS TO TORTURE ANIMALS

(Yelling "Go, girl!" at terrified creatures that don't speak English.)

Dumb Scale
Fixability Index
Outrage Level

The Situation

Every few months, civilisation puts on a little costume and pretends animal racing is a sport. Which is quite telling, really – because in most sports, both competitors know they're playing.

Here though? One gets champagne, a trophy, and a hat the size of a small country. The other gets blinkers, fear, and a chiropractor named 'Bullet'.

We line up horses and dogs like biological poker machines – pull the lever, hope the legs don't fall off, waste your shopping budget and quickly look away.

The classic line appears everywhere – on marketing brochures and cocktail napkins alike: 'They love to run'. Let's fix that shitty slogan right here and now:

Yes. They love to run. So does every toddler on Earth. Yet, strangely, no one's betting their rent money on which toddler reaches the letterbox first without tripping over and face-planting in the driveway.

Greyhounds *do* enjoy the occasional run. They also enjoy sofas, naps, gentle strolls, and not being obliged to risk life and limb chasing mechanical rabbits while random onlookers hysterically scream at them.

Why It's Ridiculous

Imagine thousands of semi-intoxicated adults in pastel outfits, shrieking at panicked animals running in circles and trying not to die on polished dirt – and no one finding this strange.

Welcome to The Melbourne Cup – or, as the horses call it 'That Annual Event Where Not All Of Us Finish'.

Greyhound racing? Same concept, just with a lower socio-economic set, smaller animals, smaller budgets, cheaper tracks and deaths that don't trend on whatever Twitter is called now. Probably because celebrity involvement is absent and the hats aren't big enough.

Greyhounds are required to race wearing muzzles. Not because they're aggressive monsters but because the industry knows what happens when terrified animals and adrenaline are forced to compete inches apart at full speed.

The muzzle isn't protection. It's damage control. And when a sport requires preventative face-restraints by default, the problem probably isn't the animals. It's the setup.

But at least the dogs are provided with a decent retirement plan which has historically included a shrug followed by a shovel to the face and a shallow patch of dirt in the bush.

Always remember: The moment we've done anything cruel long enough, it's perfectly fine to continue doing it by calling it 'nostalgic' or 'part of our culture'.

Why You Should Care

Behind every sparkling race day montage is a production line of living things we label 'excess stock'. The 'uncompetitive' ones. The 'too slow' ones. The 'ran-too-well – figured-out-the-scam-and-jumped-the-fence' ones.

Thousands are bred every year to feed the gambling industry its next miracle story. The industry breeds for winners, not homes. Which means 'too many dogs' isn't a failure of planning – it *is* the plan.

For every one 'champion', dozens are discarded like misprinted promo pens. And every on-track incident is just a polite euphemism for: "Frank – quick! We broke another one. Bring us another tarp mate".

Legal Fun Fact *(The not-so-fun kind)*

In many racing jurisdictions, greyhounds are not legally treated as companion animals at all. They are classified as *livestock* or *industry animals*.

That means fewer protections, weaker welfare laws, and a handy legal shrug when things go badly. A family dog is an individual. A racing greyhound is inventory. Same heartbeat. Different paperwork.

All of this wraps up rather simply, if inconveniently: blood sport for the 'innocent' bystanders who prefer their violence accessorised with Sunday shoes and plastic fruit stapled to their hats.

How to Un-F*ck It

There's hope. Not because humans suddenly grow hearts – that'll be asking too soon – but because they love novelty, spectacle, and pretending to be moral when someone's filming.

So here are some options:

- **Human Racing**

  Same track. Same bets. No animals. Let's see Chad from Accounts sprint 1,200 metres in crocs. Aerodynamic as a brick, but if he really wants the glory? Let him earn it.

- **Reverse Jockey Program**
  Humans carry the horses. Watch empathy rise as soon as the first three lumbar discs stack like a pile of Sunday morning pancakes.
- **Ban Greyhound Racing**
  Replace every track with a 'Dog Couch Recovery Centre'. Every ex-racer gets a sofa, unlimited snacks, and the right to nap until Earth cools down.
- **Annual Holiday: 'The Great Dismount'**
  A national holiday where, for one day, nothing with a heartbeat is put at risk for someone else's entertainment.

Leaving You With This
(Scientifically sharp, philosophically blunt, and completely pointless.)

Calling animal racing 'sport' works only if you ignore who's taking the risks. If the event requires sedatives, blinkers, or an industrial blender for the losers, it's not sport.

WTF But True

The Australian Melbourne Cup markets itself as 'The Race That Stops a Nation'. Apart from also routinely stopping a heart, in the last two decades, dozens of horses have died on 'Cup Day' and in the lead-up – legs snapped, necks shattered, lungs bursting and popping like overinflated party balloons.

Spectators cheer, refill their plastic flutes, and post #CupDayVibes while track workers swiftly roll up the grass coloured body bags behind them.

Greyhound racing isn't far behind. 'Unfit for competition' often means 'not profitable enough to keep alive'.

Thousands simply 'disappear' every year – a vanishing act with no applause and no questions. The kind of disappearance that only works if everyone agrees not to look too closely.

Against All Logic

Another Australian trainer was banned in 2023 for live-baiting greyhounds with possums. Industry spokespeople claim "a few bad apples". Truth would call it "the whole barrel's been fermenting since 1927, and at this point it's producing more 'bad apples' than cider". Apparently that headline was too wordy.

Betting Stub
(Speculatio Corporis)
*Issued to confirm a financial wager on animal performance.
Records predicted outcome, stake amount, and potential payout.
Links monetary gain to risk of injury, exhaustion,
or death of participating animals.*

Eco-Justice: Reloaded

AKA: KILLING FOR BALANCE, BUT FASHIONABLE

('Shoot the animal to save the animal' – explained by men in safari hats.)

Dumb Scale
Fixability Index
Outrage Level

The Situation

Picture it: a sun-bleached Savannah, a majestic animal, a man in khaki holding a gun as oversized as his camouflage jacket. And a well-paid camera crew standing by to immortalise the ceremonial kneel-beside-the-corpse pose.

Welcome to modern wildlife protection – where 'I love nature' somehow includes shooting a hole through it and smiling for Instagram.

The script is always the same, delivered with the confidence of someone who once skimmed a pamphlet on ecology at the airport:

- "Actually, hunting funds conservation".
- "Actually, it's population control".
- "Actually, it's necessary for balance".

- "Actually, if I say 'actually' enough times, it sounds mildly scientific".

It actually reads:

"I wanted to kill something, but I needed a story where that also made me the good guy".

At some point, we took the word 'conservation', tossed it into a mental blender, and hit purée. What came out was a stew of euphemisms so ridiculous it barely qualifies as language: 'Eco-hunters', 'ethical culls', 'sustainability permits', and the old-time favourite, 'game management' – which makes bullet holes sound like the gentle crunch of stepping onto a dry autumn leaf.

It's like appointing an arsonist to run the candle shop because he has a 'feel for the material'. And still, somehow... everyone bought the idea.

Why It's Ridiculous

The 'kill to save' philosophy is ecologically no different from decluttering your wardrobe by setting the entire house on fire.

Nature managed balance long before humans appeared with rifles, spreadsheets, and the quiet confidence of people who mistake control for 'oversight'.

Predators, drought, disease – the original biological management teams. Proof that nature was never short on balance, nor in need of armed regulators to shoot things and approve the numbers.

Hunters love to claim they're 'thinning the herd', helping nature, doing the noble thing. But somewhat, strangely, the animals they choose to *help* are always the biggest, strongest, most photogenic males – those calendar models whose dusty heads look the best mounted above a gin cabinet.

Then there's the economic argument – the safari sales pitch disguised as community development support because 'Local communities benefit'.

Yes, nothing empowers a village quite like rich tourists blasting endangered animals into oblivion so the locals can enjoy a new well.

Meanwhile, wildlife managers shuffle paperwork, juggling forms and political threats to protect animals – but not *too* many, because too many annoy wealthy landowners, whose votes seem to count disproportionately louder than most.

So off they go, inventing new phrases like children invent imaginary friends. 'Adaptive wildlife management program' – gobbledygook for 'we gave up arguing with gun lobbies' and 'we don't know how to tell people to stop shooting things, so here's a form for you to fill out'.

Naming it 'conservation' however, doesn't make it conservation. Calling a firing squad a 'sustainability team' doesn't change the outcome for the poor bastard tied to the post.

How to Un-F*ck It

- **Retire the word 'cull'**
  It's a euphemism for killing. Call it what it is; *kill*. Language decides what we're willing to excuse.
- **Invest in real conservation**
  Protect habitats, restore ecosystems, build wildlife corridors, stop fragmentation – it's the slow isolation that kills without gunfire.
- **Fund tourism, not trophies**
  Cameras shoot better, pictures last longer, cause zero funerals, and don't require bone saws, glass eyeballs, or cotton batting.
- **Use non-lethal tools when you must intervene**
  Relocation, fencing, habitat adjustments – even fertility control – applied sparingly, scientifically, and with humility. No cowboy fantasies. No quick-fix bullets. Firearms do not qualify as conservation tools.

- **Respect ecosystems as self-balancing**
  Let's all agree that more often than not, they don't need human micromanagement – they need human absence.
- **Ask before pulling the trigger**
  Would the planet explode if you didn't? If the answer isn't a hard 'yes', maybe put down the weapon, step away from the firearm and pick up a donation form instead.

Leaving You With This
(Scientifically spotless, philosophically messy, and practically useless.)

If 'death saves life', every ICU would be staffed by executioners, and morgues would be the world's most effective hospitals.

Animals are rarely in the wrong place. They're usually standing exactly where we pushed them.

Copper-Jacketed Lead Projectile
(Conservatio Letalis)
Mass-produced ammunition component.
Designed to penetrate biological tissue and cause lethality.
Used in hunting, military, and law-enforcement contexts.
Frequently described as a tool of wildlife management or conservation.

Mylk Wars

AKA: WHEN WORDS GET MORE PROTECTION THAN ANIMALS

(Deploying lawyers against almonds.)

Dumb Scale
Fixability Index
Outrage Level

The Situation

Somewhere in the bowels of the Dairy Industrial Complex, a boardroom full of very serious men with very serious ties decided the apocalypse had arrived – not by climate change, nor by public health statistics, nor by people realising cows don't exactly volunteer for the whole 'milk me daily' lifestyle – but by the sudden emergence of a carton labelled 'Oat Milk'.

Yes. Oat. Milk. Two words that, when placed together, send executives into a kind of linguistic panic, resulting in shivers and severe night sweats.

After a hundred years of selling mammary secretions extracted from animals, Big Dairy suddenly discovered its greatest rival was... *vocabulary*. It wasn't technology. Nor was it innovation. Not even consumer preference. It was a *word*.

Now they're spending millions – *millions* – of dollars lobbying governments so the public doesn't confuse almonds with animals. Because somewhere out there, according to them, is a fragile citizen thinking: "Hold on a minute... do almonds have nipples?"

Apparently this hypothetical nipple-confused shopper is the missing link – the one voter democracy must protect and tiptoe around. Precious. Vulnerable and easily bamboozled by the humble nut.

Why It's Ridiculous

If our language followed Dairy Lobby Logic – where every word must describe its literal ingredient – society would collapse under its own labels.

Hold onto your butt for the clusterfuck of everyday nonsense:

- **Peanut butter**
  No buttered peanuts at all. No udder action involved here.
- **Baby powder**
  No actual baby ingredients (we hope).
- **Hot dogs**
  Mostly lukewarm, rarely, if ever, hot tubes. Definitely not dogs.

- **Hamburgers**
  Contain no ham and aren't from Hamburg either.
- **Chicken fingers**
  The chicken had zero fingers, though they'd flip us one if they did.
- **Toothpaste**
  Contains no teeth.
- **Sausage rolls**
  That's not even a verb and answers absolutely none of the questions it raises.
- **Spam**
  No one knows what it is, and that's exactly how they like to keep it.
- **Coconut cream**
  No cows involved here, just big, brown, gentle nuts that didn't hurt anyone.

And yet the dairy lobby loses it's collective lactose over the idea of 'Almond Milk'. Suddenly, language becomes sacred scripture – and only dairy priests may interpret the word 'milk' justifiably. All nouns matter and society must be protected from accidental nut milking.
If they had their way, we'd be forced to ask for:
"One carton of nut-derived liquid, please".

Meanwhile, their own products parade around with labels like 'Happy Cow', 'Natural', and 'Farm Fresh', like the animals signed off with a hoof-print and a wink.

No, they don't mind misleading claims – just inconvenient nouns.

Why You Should Care

Because when an industry starts policing syllables, you can bet it's terrified of losing relevance *and* revenue.

Language control isn't about clarity – it's about power. It's about owning the narrative. It's about squeezing the last profitable drops from a dying business model built on a cycle of forced impregnation and stolen infancy.

Milk sales have been declining for years, and instead of adapting like a grown-up sector, dairy has chosen the emotional maturity of a toddler screaming: "That's *my* word!"

They've become the Experts of Semantics – rewriting dictionaries instead of business plans.

The agricultural equivalent of a washed-up rock band demanding the world deletes Spotify and returns to vinyl.

How to Un-F*ck It

Humans love rules? Fine. Let's give them rules:
The Literal Labels Act
All foods *must* describe themselves exactly as they are.

- **Chicken nuggets**
  Deep-fried bird lumps. Collected from a mixture of 80+ minced up chickens, combined and compressed into undefinable shapes.
- **Beef jerky**
  Dehydrated strips carved from a freshly slaughtered cow, salted, dried, and vacuum sealed for convenient snacking. Sold at every trusted service station within your local vicinity.
- **Milk**
  Mixture of mammary secretion collected from an unknown number of repeatedly impregnated cows, bottled for convenience. (Considerable amount of pus and trace amounts of industrial cleaning fluids included at no extra charge.)
- **Oat milk**
  Just plant juice really. Didn't scream at all. There's nothing to add here.

If a clearly labelled product is still mistaken for its animal-based counterpart, the issue is comprehension, not deception.

Educational support may be required, including introductory modules such as *What Is a Nut?* and *Where Do Babies Come From*.

National Campaign: *Got Context*

Because if humans can navigate phrases like 'ghosting', 'cloud storage', and 'spam' they can probably handle 'soy milk'.

Rebrand Milk As 'Breast Juice'

Suddenly watch everyone sprint to the plant milk aisle.

Leaving You With This
(Scientifically accurate, philosophically strange, and mentally inconvenient.)

The real reason the dairy lobby fears plant milk? It doesn't require:

- perpetual pregnancy,
- newborn removal,
- industrial milking machinery,
- an endless supply of antibiotics and resources.

It just requires... well, oats or almonds really. That however, is hard to compete with when your business model involves removing new born babies and slaughtering the unwanted males at birth.

Almonds – in general don't scream or kick or cry for their offspring. They just – grow there. Quietly. Indifferently. A level of calm that terrifies industries. A true emerging threat to the empire indeed.

WTF But True

In 2017, the European Court of Justice actually ruled that the word 'Milk' could *only* refer to animal-derived liquid. Which means 'almond milk' became 'almond drink'.

Meanwhile, in the US, lawmakers introduced the *Dairy Pride Act*, which basically says: "Think of the poor word 'Milk' – won't someone protect it?" Truly, a heroic stand, apparently – for a noun.

Against All Logic

When asked why people prefer plant milks, one dairy lobbyist boldly answered:
"They're being misled by clever marketing".

Yes indeed. Clever marketing. The very thing dairy has been doing since the first carton featured a cartoon cow enjoying a meadow that exists exclusively in the illustrator's imagination.

If the Mylk Wars teach us anything at all, it's this: Humans will fight to the death to protect their favourite words, even while ignoring the suffering of the animals behind the ones they use the most.

Plant-Based Cheese Packaging
(Lex Lactis Defensiva)
Commercial food product labelled using an alternative spelling.
Produced to resemble conventional cheese in form and use.
Naming is adjusted to comply with existing food labelling regulations.

Feeding Frenzy

AKA: Gluttony – Served With Extra Fries

(Snacking our way to extinction.)

Dumb Scale
Fixability Index
Outrage Level

The Situation

Let's talk chubby!

The only species capable of dying from too much food while simultaneously complaining we've got nothing in the fridge. Squirrels hoard nuts. We hoard snacks in industrial-sized Tupperware containers.

We don't hunt because we're hungry – we hunt because Netflix paused to buffer and gave us three seconds to remember the fridge is only eight steps away.

Somewhere along the evolutionary buffet line, survival became self-indulgence. We stopped eating to live and started living to chew.

Our ancestors fought famine. We fight the urge to buy a third air fryer because this one 'circulates the air around your fries more evenly' while playing soothing tunes via its built-in WiFi.

And though we love to announce to the world that we have 'gone vegan', organic, and cruelty-free, we're still shovelling enough calories down to feed an African mid-sized village and its goats.

Common forms of modern gluttony:
- **Snackation**
  A 3-hour round trip from couch to fridge. Souvenirs include minor guilt, a trail of chocolate stains on your shirt and crumbs on the floor.
- **Emotional eating**
  Caloric self-soothing in lieu of emotional processing. Basically therapy without leaving the couch, but meltier and softer and with extra cream and sugar.
- **Vegan buffet**
  The resource footprint of a small orbiting moon, just with more chickpeas and moral righteousness.
- **Supersizing**
  Because 'environmental responsibility', looks a lot like like washing down the fries with a 1.5 litre bottle of carbonated sugar water.
- **Food waste**
  Buying six avocados because you're 'definitely becoming a smoothie person this week'. Five will die noble but mushy deaths at the back of the kitchen counter.

Why It's Ridiculous

Humans brag about saving the rainforest, then consume enough imported calories to re-burn it – before posting twelve-plate-deep, plant-based brunch photos, tagged #sustainable, as if that offsets the truck's diesel emissions delivering the quinoa.

Meanwhile, forests are bulldozed to grow more soy, almonds, mangoes, blueberries – not for the starving, but for the freshly overstuffed and because some human specimens discovered that appetite can also be turned into a hobby.

Let's call it what it is, my well-fed friends: gluttony. Greed stuffed into a greasy bib, steam-rolling ecosystems faster than you can fill your plate for seconds.

Why You Should Care

Every unnecessary mouthful consumes something else.

- More food demand → more farmland.
- More farmland → fewer forests.
- Fewer forests → fewer animals.

Simple. Brutal. And unless we've invented a parallel planet to grow food on – non-negotiable.

It's not just cows and pigs paying the price – it's elephants, amphibians, pollinators, and anything unlucky enough to need a tree whose habitat gets converted into someone's light afternoon snack.

While humans hoard calories, wildlife starves for space. A single nation's food waste could feed billions of non-human mouths, but instead it generates methane and fat landfill gulls.

We don't just eat beyond our means – we eat beyond our species.

Ethics isn't just about what sits on the plate. It's also about who lost their habitat for five seconds of taste-bud tingles, followed by "Oh my god, I am sooo full", inevitably ending with the quiet loosening of the upper pants button.

How to Un-F*ck It

- Eat like the planet's *invited* to dinner – not like it's an all-nighter at Sizzlers.
- Redefine 'enough' as a standard of decency.
- Turn 'portion control' into planetary control.
- Treat food waste as a minor social offence – corrected through mandatory composting and public accountability.
- Holiday calorie caps. Or at least solid fines for the plate lickers who say "just a taste" five times and then attack the pavlova when no-one is looking.

- Before ordering dessert, ask yourself: Who's really paying for *this* extra slice?

Leaving You With This
(Scientifically supported, karmically inconvenient, and 100% gluten-free.)

Gluttony isn't loud. It doesn't roar. It whispers: "Go on. Just one more bite". Civilisations rarely fall from famine anymore. They fall from 'seconds'.

Hunger, divorced from need, is the quiet driver no one wants to mention, because it lives in the mirror. It doesn't just double the waistline. It doubles the impact on everything.

WTF But True

- People in wealthy nations consume nearly *double* the calories required for health. That's double the crops, double the land, double the habitats erased.
- Roughly one-third of all food produced globally is wasted – about 1.3 billion tonnes a year. Enough to feed every hungry human and several billion other creatures.
- Over-consumption is now a leading indirect driver of species extinction. Yes – gluttony kills, with a soup-stained napkin.

- At this rate, 'just one more bite' is a gigantic public health bill expenditure and warming up to become quietly an extinction-level event.

XXL Drink Cup
(Abundantia Normalisata)
Disposable container designed to hold large volumes of sweetened beverages.
Enables consumption at quantities
exceeding typical dietary recommendations.
Commonly paired with calorie-dense meals.

Shell Shock

AKA: Eggscuses, Eggscuses, Everywhere
(Egged into ignorance.)

Dumb Scale
Fixability Index
Outrage Level

The Situation

Welcome to the sunny-side-up nightmare, where the yolk is bright and the smiles are fake. The egg industry – that wholesome, farm-fresh fantasy of rolling hills, cartoon hens, and labels designed to preserve a childhood illusion – is in reality one of the most efficient cruelty systems ever engineered by a species with opposable thumbs and selective empathy.

Let's start with the punchline that somehow never makes it onto the egg carton label: Every year, *billions* of day-old male chicks are ground up alive in industrial macerators.

For the layperson, these figures may sound confusing. So let's go through the numbers again. Not 'many'. Not 'some'. *Billions*.

That translates to roughly 700,000 to 800,000 chicks *every hour*, before we even begin counting chickens raised long enough to be eaten.

Just the routine cost of our breakfast.

Because in the logic of the industry, males are the equivalent of biological office clutter – they don't lay eggs, so into the blender they go.

Some are lucky to be gassed first, which is considered the humane option – a process that involves suffocating the baby birds before grinding them into mulch, then converting the sludge into pet food for Rover or your 'natural organic' backyard fertiliser. No life goes to waste at EggCo™.

If this all sounds too familiar, it's because 'Soylent Green' now reads less like dystopia and more like a business model awaiting government approval.

But let's talk about the hens – the actual egg machines of the industry. Generously provided with a reusable, free battery cage – a little smaller than the footprint of your laptop. Minds erode. Bones break. Bodies learn to bend into new, and very wrong shapes.

And there they stay, spending their short life stacked in metal filing cabinets stuffed with ammonia, misery, and that unmistakable scent of executives and stockholders unable to pronounce the words 'sentience' or 'ethics'.

But wait – Australia, like every country that considers itself civilised and clings to a conscience, has a solution: 'Free-range'. Or as this book will proudly rename it: 'Free-Range-ish'. You know, that system where hens roam, in the same way you 'roam' when the plane lands but the seat-belt sign stays on.

"But how can you say this?" you might ask – and rightfully so – because after all, we have the industry's crown jewel: an **RSPC**-*ish (**R**esponsible **S**ociety for **P**retending **C**ruelty is **A**lright)* certified label slapped on the egg carton.

A label that sounds comfortingly familiar to an Australian animal welfare organisation we absolutely won't name, yet somehow ends up approving farms where chickens live the kind of life you'd report *to* the RSPCA.

The label that whispers comfort into guilty consumers' ears, a tiny colourful cartoon hen perched on your conscience, pecking you on the cheek and saying, "Shh..shh... don't think too hard", while humming a corporate lullaby.

A comforting fiction in which chickens participate willingly in the process.

They don't.

What actually happens is simple: Hens are bred, confined, exploited, and discarded once their production declines – shipped to slaughter at a fraction of their natural lifespan.

The 'ethical' version still kills them. Just more politely, with a smile, and a cute chicken logo on the pack.

Why It's Ridiculous

Egg-industry logic belongs to the category of practices humanity was supposed to outgrow. Each argument is a carefully constructed exercise in avoidance.

- **Chickens don't mind laying eggs**
  Right – distress is easy to dismiss when you've already decided it doesn't count.
- **Free-range hens live good lives**
  Freedom, here, is just a word. Beak-tips are clipped or burned off. Crowding remains. Slaughter follows declining output.
- **Eggs are natural**
  So are floods, parasites, disease, and lions eating tourists off safari buses. Nature *explains* reality. It doesn't define ethics.
- **It's tradition**
  Humanity clings to eggs with the devotion of someone refusing to let go of a toxic ex. We don't *need* eggs. We like the *ritual* – the power of breaking something at breakfast, something that was once

whole so the day feels normal again. Just a little cruelty sprinkled on top of our toast, sunny-side up.

How to Un-F*ck It

- **Ditch the egg marketing fantasy**
  If a product needs cartoon chickens to sell it, something's being hidden – probably reality.
- **Stop rewarding cruelty with nostalgia**
  If your morning ritual begins with a casualty, it shouldn't be classed as breakfast.
- **Support real migratory alternatives**
  Plant-based eggs, tofu scrambles, mung-bean magic – the future can be conveniently delicious.
- **Expose the euphemisms**
  'Free-range-ish', 'Happy-Farm Approved', 'Enriched colony housing' – poems written by those employed to obscure reality.
- **Adopt moral consistency**
  If killing male chicks horrifies you, don't support the system that depends on it.
- **Ask the big question**
  If your breakfast raises moral questions – maybe just try some toast until you work out why.

Leaving You With This
(Scientifically inflated, philosophically punctured, and spiritually flat.)

If the happiness displayed on the carton were real, the industry would just *show* you the farm. They'd livestream it. They'd brag about it. But instead, all you get is a carton, a cute logo, and a silence loud enough to hear the slow footprints of your conscience circling the inside of your skull.

Egg Cup
(Innocentia Domestica)
Small tableware item designed to support a single cooked
chicken egg during consumption.
Used in domestic and commercial dining settings.
Associated with egg-based food practices.

Udder Nonsense

AKA: THE DARK SIDE OF THE MOO

(The industrialisation of another mammal's lactation fluids.)

Dumb Scale
Fixability Index
Outrage Level

(This chapter may be skipped by anyone with an uncle who runs a small, humane dairy farm where cows are kissed goodnight like pets, lovingly named, produce milk indefinitely without impregnation, and are still mysteriously replaced every few years.)

The Situation

Somewhere in prehistory, some guy watched a calf nursing and thought, "Yeah... I get in on that".

And nobody stopped him. Humanity, once again in its infinite acceptance, nodded along like this was perfectly reasonable behaviour. Not one person asked "Why?" or the more appropriate, "Mate... you okay?"

Fast-forward a few thousand years and here we are, squeezing the nipples of another species to obtain their boob juice – foaming it, churning it, fermenting it, and drizzling it over everything from cereal to spaghetti.

The behaviour itself requires no additional context.

We don't even flinch anymore; the absurdity has been grandfathered in. Drinking the bodily secretions of a four-stomached mammal no longer classifies as strange.

Let's demystify the surprisingly wide variety of bovine fluid worship:

- **Milk**
  Body fluids, sipped or soaked up with cookies – because nothing screams childhood like a warm glass of slimy secretions.
- **Cheese**
  Mammary lacteal solution, reworked into hard, soft, yellow, white, and blue – stringy, sometimes mouldy disks or rectangular cubes. Familiarity *has* to do the rest.
- **Butter**
  Fat-slab of churned glandular fluids. Spread it on a cracker, eat it and pretend it's normal.
- **Yoghurt**
  Fermented cow mucus – now in mango flavour! Because what yoghurt *really* needed was that missing tropical flair.
- **Ice Cream**
  Frozen breast milk – shaped like popsicles. For kids. For birthdays – to refresh.

Why It's Ridiculous

An entire industry sponsoring national food pyramids built on the idea that stealing and sipping on another species' baby food turns you into a strong adult.

Celebrity chefs analyse cheese like something that died in a cellar twelve months ago and now costs $38 a slice. *Holy udder!*

Shopping centre fridge shelves reserved for udder slop in *fourteen* varieties: full cream, half cream, light, skim, extra calcium, whatever A2 is supposed to be and of course lactose-free – none of the lactose – all of the cruelty.

Somehow squeezing our *own* nipples felt too weird, so we outsourced.

Why You Should Care

Behind the happy-cow barnyard charm sits CowCo™ – a farm-fresh company that prides itself on perfecting the art of industrial optimism: the ability to smile warmly while frankly, doing – quite horrific things.

With family-friendly slogans like: 'Turning motherhood into a body-fluid supply chain', printed in Comic Sans font cheerful enough to distract from the meaning.

Cows aren't bred anymore – they're 'scheduled into pregnancy'. Their calves aren't born – they're 'allocated'.

And within hours, newborns are selected and sorted into a two-track career system:

- **Females**
  Inducted into the Prestigious Lactation Program – mandatory participation, indefinite duration.
- **Males**
  Routed to the 'Limited-Time Opportunity Division' – a role defined by immediate termination.
  Benefits include one lungful of fresh air, the possibility of a brief sunbeam (weather permitting), and a short scenic stroll to nowhere in particular before permanent retirement through the exit, passing the double barrel bolt gun nobody mentions.[4]

Eventually, once a cow's milk quota drops, she's thanked for her service by being turned into a discounted fast-food patty – the final act in a career of forced generosity. Because nothing says "We value you" like a $4 combo meal at Maccas during your 30 minute lunch break.

But what about 'family-friendly' farming? That phrase does a lot of heavy, hernia-inducing lifting here, considering what it is trying to describe.

Then there's the environmental carnage: rivers – *actual rivers* – of manure leaking into waterways,

---

4   Animal welfare is our top priority.

creating dead zones that make the Great Barrier Reef look like the Gold Coast after a schoolies weekend. (And for those unfamiliar with that area: it's *not* a compliment).

As a bonus, add in methane, CO_2, deforestation, and basic ecosystem collapse. All so brand-loyal consumers can keep their coffee frothy, cheese platters photogenic, and quarter-pounders cheap. We're not just milking cows. We're milking the planet dry.

How to Un-F*ck It

Rename all dairy with clinical honesty – because euphemisms had a good run for way too long:

- **New coffee size**
  Medium, Large, and 'Trauma' (for those who realise mid-sip what's actually in their cup).
- **Milk**
  Cross-species mammary secretion, harvested post-pregnancy, combined from multiple animals and marketed as 'nutritious', 'refreshing' and 'necessary for good health'.
- **Cheese**
  Hardened, aged bovine body-fluid, solidified paste – adored globally for reasons nobody can quite adequately explain anymore.

- **Yoghurt**
  Spoonable udder residue, marketed as 'gut health' – a clever rebranding term for 'controlled bacterial growth'.
- **The 'National Day of Dairy Silence'**
  A 24-hour break from cow's milk, cheese, yoghurt, and creamy sauces. A moment to reflect... and try not to sob into your oat milk latte.

Leaving You With This
(Scientifically crunchy, philosophically leaky, and morally damp.)

Keep your lips off cow tits. You're better than this. Probably.

WTF But True

Roughly 65% of the human specimen is lactose intolerant – meaning the normal biological response to dairy is: *don't*. And still, the crowds are guzzling down the slimy fluids like a cask of cheap wine on a Saturday Netflix night.

Against All Odds

Japan – land of samurai, kaiju, and Godzilla's favourite stomping ground – lived dairy-free for *centuries*. The Samurai still kicked arse in full armour. Milk did not make the blade.

Domestic Dairy Cow *(Holstein-Friesian)*
(Extractio Continua)
Domesticated bovine bred for milk production.
Artificially inseminated to sustain lactation.
Milk extracted mechanically on a regular schedule.
Offspring removed shortly after birth.
Average productive lifespan: 4–6 years.

The Silence of the Ham

AKA: When Justice Got a Muzzle

(How 'Ag-Gag' laws made caring illegal.)

Dumb Scale
Fixability Index
Outrage Level

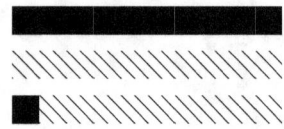

The Situation

Once upon a time, a person with more courage than common sense slipped a camera into a slaughterhouse. And shocker: the footage did not resemble a wellness retreat for pigs. It wasn't pastoral. It wasn't humane. It wasn't even sanitary half the time. It was *reality*. And reality, as it tends to do, embarrassed the hell out of the meat industry.

What followed was immediate.

The internet lost its collective mind. Politicians squirmed. Farmers fumed. The meat industry reps screamed **"UNFAIR!"**, and lawmakers nodded like obedient waiters taking a steak order. Ever eager to protect the feelings of corporations – they nodded politely and said, "Yes, of course... we should absolutely criminalise honesty".

Enter the birth of the Ag-Gag laws. Or, as we call them in Australia: 'biosecurity laws', because 'don't film this' didn't sound official enough.

The grand tradition of shooting the messenger, burying the evidence, then making it illegal to mention the hole in the ground. These laws don't stop cruelty. They stop *witnessing* cruelty.

Notice how Ag-Gag laws never show up at strawberry farms? Nobody's been dragged to court for live-streaming their YouTube walk through an apple orchard. You can film a thousand hectares of lettuce growing in HD and the government won't twitch. But point a camera at a pig in distress and suddenly you're one sneeze away from being branded a bio-terrorist.

You can legally kill the animal – but if you film the killing, you're the threat to public order.

It's like outlawing mirrors because they keep showing the truth. Rude!

Undercover investigation was rebranded into 'bio-terrorism'. Whistle-blowers became 'trespassers'. And truth? Truth got ground, bleached, shrink-wrapped, and stuck with a label that says 'Not For Public Consumption'.

Why It's Ridiculous

Imagine going to a restaurant where they hand you a blindfold and say, "Just trust us. Everything's clean".

Then the owner lobbies Parliament to make it illegal to take that blindfold off. That's your Government approved Ag-Gag in a nutshell – a sweaty, panicked nutshell.

The official excuse? 'Bio-Security'. Because nothing spreads disease faster than... truth? The only field where disease outbreaks are fine, but honesty is a hazard.

Compassion, too, apparently. Can't have that floating around unchecked. People might start feeling things and acting morally – disastrous for the corporate profit margins.

The real reason is simpler – and greasier: Money. It's vastly cheaper to hide cruelty than to fix it. Ag-Gag laws didn't appear because farmers needed protection. They appeared because customers who saw what was happening inside factory farms started saying, "Yeah... naaa.... thanks", and the industry reacted the way a teenager does when you catch them minimising three browser tabs at once: panic, delete, deny.

The narrative shifted overnight: Suddenly the problem wasn't violence – it was *filming* violence. Not suffering – but *documenting* suffering. Cruelty was never the scandal – visibility was.

A society that worships free speech discovered there was one phrase too dangerous to allow: 'Look'.

How to Un-F*ck It

- **Call it what it is**
  State sponsored censorship wrapped in work boots, corporate perfume and wearing a high-vis vest of bullshit.

- **Back the truth-tellers**
  Support investigative journalists, whistle-blowers, and anyone brave enough to enter a slaughterhouse with anything other than a bolt-gun and a mop.

- **Vote with a conscience**
  Pretend empathy is a renewable resource – because it is – and vote for people who recognise that.

- **Share the footage**
  If truth makes you uncomfortable, that means it's working. Truth isn't supposed to tuck you in at night; it's supposed to yank the blanket.

- **Question the 'protect the farmer' narrative**
  Which farmer, exactly? The family running a modest little operation... or the multinational empire with more lawyers than livestock?

- **Less gag orders, more mirrors**
  Let the world see what the system wants hidden. Darkness only wins when it's left unchallenged.

Leaving You With This
(Scientifically magnetic, philosophically repellent, and socially awkward.)

If slaughterhouses had glass walls, there'd be fewer barbecue festivals and more therapy sessions.

Ag-Gag laws turned glass walls into one-way mirrors: the public sees nothing, and the industry watches everything. We deserve more than that – we deserve transparency of our food system.

No Filming Sign
(Obscuratio Legalis)
Industrial signage material displayed at agricultural facilities
involving animal confinement and slaughter.
Used to restrict recording of legally sanctioned procedures.
Violation may result in criminal penalties.

The Kid's Menu

AKA: Fine Dining on Infancy

(A taste for animals who haven't reached maturity.)

Dumb Scale
Fixability Index
Outrage Level

(We finally meet the devil – and it is us.)

The Situation

There are scandals society will tolerate – political corruption, celebrity apologies clearly drafted by someone who wasn't in the room when the scandal happened, billionaires pretending to pay tax – but there's another truth so uncomfortable, so wildly grotesque, that our society hides it behind recipe books and barbecue smoke.

We are, quite literally, a civilisation that snacks on infants and calls it 'a balanced diet'.

Not metaphorical babies. Not symbolic babies. *Actual* infants of other species – slaughtered before their childhoods even begin.

Let's consult the Great Livestock Registry of Psychopathy, shall we?

- **Chickens**
  Natural lifespan: 8–12 years.
  Slaughtered at 6 weeks.
- **Pigs**
  Natural lifespan: 15–20 years.
  Slaughtered at 5–6 months.
- **Lambs**
  Natural lifespan: 12–14 years.
  Slaughtered at 4–8 months.
- **Calves** *(veal)*
  Natural lifespan: 20–25 years.
  Slaughtered for veal at a few *days* to a few months.
- **Turkeys**
  Natural lifespan: 10 years.
  Slaughtered at 12–20 weeks.

None of them are allowed to grow up.

Humanity proudly calls itself civilised while routinely eating beings who, by our own standards, are still children.

And then we invented the masterstroke: we rebrand the violence. Lamb becomes 'tender', veal becomes 'delicate', chicken becomes 'light meat' – euphemisms designed to turn age into marketing.

Civilisation's culinary legacy is a maternity ward with a drive-through window.

Why It's Ridiculous

Only Homo sapiens could take the concept of infancy – something we normally go to extreme lengths to protect – and turn it into a delicacy if it happens to belong to another species.

When questioned, the justification is always simple: "The meat is more tender".

Tender. Not delicious. Not nutritious. *Tender.* As in: soft enough for your conscience to slip right through it and without leaving a dent, pretending we're not monsters.

And the hypocrisy is remarkable. We agonise over the emotional well-being of pets. A lamb slaughtered before its first birthday? Pass the mint sauce.

Meanwhile, supermarkets politely avoid telling you that 'free-range pork belly' is a baby's belly. That 'buttermilk chicken strips' come from someone who never learned to scratch the dirt. And that a 'rack of lamb' is youth turned into garnish.

And just when you think the baby-eating menu couldn't get any darker, a dish so bleak it makes your conscience lean over and whisper, "Surely not": a dish where a newborn is taken from its mother, killed before it learns to stand properly, and then cooked in the very milk that was supposed to keep it alive.[5]

This is one of those dishes that makes even hardened chefs stop mid-stir, question their career choice and whisper to themselves: "Mate... what the actual hell are you doing here?"

We've normalised it so completely that defending infant slaughter barely raises an eyebrow. "Humans have always eaten meat", they say, using history to excuse whatever is on the menu, while turning adolescence into appetisers.

We didn't just lose the plot – we seasoned it, crumbed it, and deep-fried it; then posted it on Instagram with a filter that makes the cooked young flesh pop like a holiday sunset.

How to Un-F*ck It

- **Call babies by their real names**
  Lambs are babies. Chicks are babies. Piglets are babies. If it's young enough to be marketed as adorable or feature in a children's book, it's too young to end up on your plate.
- **Stop hiding the killing of the young**
  'Tender', 'delicate', 'mild flavour', 'white meat' – language designed to make age sound appetising.

---

5   Animal welfare is our top priority.

- **Let animals grow up**
  If a creature's natural lifespan is twenty years, maybe we let it live past twenty weeks, as radical as this may sound.
- **Stop pretending this is tradition**
  No culture has ever matured by consuming its young. It's usually the last stage before collapse.

Leaving You With This
(Scientifically polite, philosophically rude, and socially confusing.)

The animal agriculture industry depends on animals staying abstract and their suffering staying unseen. When either one becomes visible, the knife gets very, very heavy.

Milk Feeding Bottle *(Industrial unit)*
(Cura Substituta)
Injection-moulded plastic vessel fitted with a rubber teat.
Used to administer milk formula to juvenile livestock
following maternal separation.
Commonly deployed in dairy, veal, and lamb production systems.

BREAKING NEWS
Planet Thrives in Post-Meat Era
Global News Network – December 23, 2048

It has been just over twenty years since the world began its historic transition away from animal agriculture. Today, the results are undeniable: the planet is breathing easier, oceans are replenished, and humanity is healthier than ever.

In 2025, less than one percent of the Planet's population identified as vegan. Meat and dairy industries were considered untouchable giants, supplying trillions of calories at the expense of land, water, and animal lives.

Few could have imagined that within two decades those same industries would close their doors, relics of a bygone age.

The last slaughterhouse in the United States shut down in 2039. In Europe, dairy subsidies were redirected toward oat, soy, and lupin cooperatives. Australia recently declared 'complete agricultural regeneration', with vast former grazing land now restored to native bushland. Satellite images confirm a thirty percent recovery of global forest cover compared to 2025.

Oceans, once over-fished to collapse, are teeming again. Marine scientists report whale populations at their highest levels in centuries, while coral reefs – once written off as doomed – show remarkable regeneration thanks to reduced pollution and stabilised temperatures.

Public health data are equally striking. Heart disease and type-2 diabetes, long associated with diets heavy in animal products, have declined so sharply that the World Health Organisation recently closed its dedicated monitoring division. Average human lifespans have increased by nearly seven years since 2025.

A parallel shift occurred not just in what the world ate, but how much. The 2038 'Enough Is Plenty' accord – initially dismissed as symbolic – quietly rewired global consumption norms. Average calorie intake fell by more than a third, while global food waste was cut nearly in half. The result was not scarcity, but surplus: enough food, enough land, enough room to breathe.

More than twelve million square kilometres of former farmland have since begun returning to functional ecosystems. Rewilding projects across South America, Southeast Asia, Europe, and Australia report the return of species absent for generations. Obesity and diet-related illnesses have declined for the first time in over a century, a reversal health authorities attribute to a cultural recalibration rather than medical intervention.
As one environmental economist noted, the breakthrough was not technological but philosophical: civilisation discovered that enough was indeed plenty.

Former meat corporations didn't vanish; they reinvented. The world's largest former beef processor now produces high-protein chickpea flour. Dairy conglomerates pivoted to precision-fermented milk proteins, indistinguishable from their predecessors and cruelty-free. Economists point to this as 'the smoothest industrial revolution in human history'.

Critics once warned of protein shortages and cultural collapse. Instead, kitchens flourished. Today's global cuisine is richer and more diverse than ever, celebrating lentils in Lagos, jackfruit in Jakarta, hemp in Hamburg, and lab-crafted Brie in Paris.

"Twenty years ago, veganism was dismissed as fringe", said UN Secretary-General Acnica Pactel. "Today, it is simply normal. Humanity has shown that when we align our plates with our morals and with our planet, we can quite literally save the world".

The Last Bendy Straw
(Sacrificium Symbolicum)
Single-use plastic drinking implement.
Designed with an articulated bend to assist liquid consumption.
Commonly distributed with beverages in food service settings.
Recently discovered and donated for viewing.

On Numbers and Other Distractions
PENCILS READY. FOR THE FACT-CHECK ENTHUSIASTS.

(Because someone, somewhere, will still send an email.)

Before someone clears their throat to point out that the recommended protein intake is technically 0.82g per kilo of bodyweight, not 0.80g, or that abandoned fishing gear accounts for 42% rather than 46%, let's pause for a moment. This isn't a PhD thesis. It's a philosophical slap in the face.

Your face.

This book isn't about decimals; it's about delusion. It doesn't claim scientific infallibility – it claims that maybe, just maybe, humanity should stop eating, breeding, and bulldozing with the cheerful efficiency of institutionalised destruction.

So, yes, relax, we all know that:

- some data sources surely differ.
- figures *will* and do fluctuate.
- statistics evolve faster than climate denial.

But remember, while you're busy Googling, the planet's still on fire – and the animals aren't holding calculators in their paws, claws, fins, or whatever evolutionary workaround they were issued instead of thumbs.

Now, to clarify: If a joke offended you, it probably wasn't aimed *at* you. If a number baffled you, the work's done.

And if your main concern is the rounding error in a world collapsing from excess – you've missed the point entirely.

Let's not get lost in spreadsheets. Whether livestock occupies just under or just over 80% of global farmland, or whether we macerate 700,000 or 650,000 baby chicks per hour, the result is the same. The issue isn't arithmetic. It's apathy.

So yes, call it exaggeration if it helps you sleep. But every punchline in this book rests on a truth so absurd it barely needed any inflation at all.

And now, the final disclaimer:

All nitpicking complaints will be published, printed on recycled paper and, when convenient, read aloud to rescued cows for their entertainment during grazing periods. Highlights may also be shared on social media for the amusement of humans currently grazing elsewhere.

If precision is your refuge while the world burns, this appendix was written for you. The rest of the book was written for everyone else.

C.K.

To Those Who Lit the Fire
AND A FEW BRAVE HEROES TRYING TO PUT IT OUT

(This book would not exist without these people.)

- To the **RSPCA** – tireless defenders of pets, selective defenders of farmed animals, and world-class champions of "We'll save the dog, but good luck to the pig".
  Without their majestic double standards, this book would have lacked a character arc and the people of the world would have to deal with non-approved egg cartons.
- To the **Dairy Industry** – whose marketing team managed the extraordinary feat of convincing entire nations that lactating mammals produce 'healthy drinks' for unrelated species. Your commitment to udder nonsense gave these pages their calcium-fortified rage.
- To the **Australian Government** – for pioneering the Ag-Gag laws that bravely demonstrated how to silence truth in a democracy while keeping a straight face. A masterclass in, "Move along, nothing ethical is happening here".
- To **Big Meat Advertising** – for proving you can mass-market and sell anything with enough fire, smoke, and a man growling at a barbecue, pretending this is what normal adulthood looks like now.

Your commitment to this propaganda kept the satire supplied for months.

- To **Influencers Who Eat Raw Liver** on Camera – Thank you for reminding us that evolution is not a straight line. Your work in the field of nutritional performance art will certainly be studied by future anthropologists and classified under 'Humanity's Weirdest Behaviours'.
- To **The Term 'Humane Slaughter'** – poetry. Pure poetry. A linguistic origami swan made entirely of denial. This book is forever in your debt.
- To **Everyone Who Said 'But Plants Feel Pain'** – your dedication to philosophical gymnastics would shame an Olympic squad. If mental back-flips burned calories, you'd all be anorexic.
- To the **Fishing Industry** – for rebranding 'slow suffocation by air' as 'family bonding'. Truly, nothing says 'love' louder than watching a sentient being drown on land while your dad cracks open a can of beer.
- To the **Deniers** – for calmly disputing the existence of a fire while standing in what used to be a patio. The smoke is real, the heat is measurable, and the denial is... impressive.
- To **Supermarkets** – for placing bacon next to cartoon pigs smiling on the packaging. It's comforting, in a deeply unsettling way.

- To **Every Person Who Asked "But Where Do You Get Your Protein?"** – thank you for your consistency. Like magpies in August, you can always be relied upon to swoop at the worst possible moment.

- To **Earthling Ed**
  For dismantling carnivorous logic with calm, patience, and an almost unreasonable commitment to reason.
- To **Joey Carbstrong**
  For bringing moral clarity into public debate with a refusal to soften it for comfort.
- To **Dr Michael Greger**
  For treating nutrition as a matter of consequence, not lifestyle. And for maintaining unwavering enthusiasm in a world determined to ignore both the consequences and the cause.
- To **The Creators of *Dominion***
  For showing the world what really happens behind the curtains – because apparently society needed a feature-length horror film to remind them where their food comes from, before reconsidering chicken nuggets.

- To **Erin Janus** (*Dairy Is Scary*)
  For compressing an entire industry's reality into five minutes, without so much as raising her voice.
- To **Seb Alex**
  For teaching activism with the clarity of a physics lecture and the charm of someone who still believes humans might evolve empathy on purpose.
- To **Gary Yourofsky**
  For dragging animal rights into the spotlight with uncompromising moral force, saying what others wouldn't, and proving that one human with conviction can shake an entire culture – even if the weight of that fight eventually demanded everything in return.
- To **Ingrid Newkirk** and **PETA**
  For the relentless, unapologetic reminder that animals aren't props, products, or emotional support sausages.
- To the **'Anonymous for the Voiceless'** volunteers
  For standing in the streets, screens in hand, hearts wide open, inviting strangers to look – really look – at the lives behind their dinner plates.
- To the doctors, dietitians, and nutritionists of **Plant-Based News, NutritionFacts,** and beyond

For doing the math, writing the papers, citing the sources, and generally making this book sound far smarter than it had any right to be.

- To **Every Activist** who has no fame
  For chalking footpaths, rescuing hens, leafleting in the rain, editing footage at 3am, and doing it again tomorrow.
- **And finally**
  To every educator, documentarian and activist who provided the facts, the courage, and the moral guidance for this book – thank you for doing the legwork while the rest of the world argued about protein.

The Museum Of Human History
Yesterday's Artefacts

Former Exhibit
(Absentia Consequens)
Removed following changes in human behaviour.
(intentionally left empty)

You've seen enough.
What happens next is yours to decide.

thevegansarecoming.com.au